Beyond O

Betsy Blankenbaker

Published in 2017

by Beautiful Infinity Books

USA

Cover Design by Paul Yinger

ISBN 978-0692873250

CONTENTS

For my mother, Virginia

For my granddaughter, Sunny

*And for my daughter, Lucy, who encouraged me to
break the silence.*

"I want to write a novel about Silence," he said;

"the things people don't say."

- Virginia Woolf, The Voyage Out

INTRODUCTION

When I was a child, I didn't mind going to the dentist because we had a family dentist who sang to us through our appointments. When I was ten, I remember laughing as the doctor broke into a Neil Diamond tune as he started the drill to begin filling a cavity. A few minutes earlier, an assistant stuck a long needle deep inside my mouth to numb me but apparently the pain medicine was not enough because when the doctor started drilling, a shock went through my tooth and down my spine. I must have flinched because the doctor looked at me and sang, "Are you okay?" My eyes said no but I nodded my head yes. It was the early 1970s and I'd learned to be nice and to not question authority. It was one of the many times I stayed silent when I was in pain. I heard the high pitch whir of the drill get louder as the doctor continued. I squeezed my eyes shut and counted slowly to ten knowing I could tolerate anything for ten seconds. When I got to ten and he was still drilling, I started to count again. "One, two, three, four..." My eyes grew moist with tears. The doctor sang louder.

The first time I stayed silent, I was six. After a teenage neighbor molested me in my childhood bedroom, I ran passed my mom in the kitchen and outside into the yard. I knew something bad had happened. I was too afraid to speak up. That was the first time I felt unsafe in my body, but not the last time.

I stayed quiet for the next forty years. I allowed the trauma to silence me.

"Muriel Rukeyser asks, 'What would happen if one woman told the truth about her life? The world would split open.' Betsy Blankenbaker did the thing I haven't read anyone else do before. She said all the things out loud."

— Rochelle Schieck, Qoya

In 2014, I released a book about spending five years healing my body after a lifetime of sexual assault and harassment. *Autobiography of an Orgasm* opened with the line, "I had my first orgasm when I was thirty-six, which means I spent half my life faking it," and for the next 40,000 words, I wrote all the ways my body shut down after abuse.

It was a relief to write the truth. Writing about the trauma and how it impacted my orgasm and my voice was a way to take the shame away from my body's natural ability to express itself. Telling the truth was an act of liberation.

After releasing the book something unexpected happened—I began to receive story after story from readers who thanked me for putting words to their own disconnection from their sensual energy. For some, it became a starting point to look at their relationships to their bodies. For others, it became a launching point for respecting their bodies as sacred and even experiencing healing through orgasm.

As I was completing this book, social networking and the media were flooded with messages of women saying "Me too" about experiencing sexual assault in Hollywood and beyond. Women were speaking up about sexual harassment and abuse in bigger numbers than ever.

We can't change the past, but as women living in a western culture who have more rights than other women around the world, it is a public service for us to speak up for ourselves, for our daughters, for our mothers and grandmothers who may have stayed silent.

This book is the story of initiating and reclaiming my body and life through honoring my sensual energy, the same energy some men, religions, and multiple assaults have tried to cut me off from.

We live on an earth full of wonders and sacred places. I took my search closer to home to discover the wonders of my body after a lifetime of ignoring it. Through my commitment to explore the sacred land within in my vagina and my womb, I discovered the mysterious life force that exists within the darkness.

Betsy Blankenbaker

NOTE TO READERS

This work is a memoir. It reflects the author's present recollection of her life. Certain names, places, events and identifying characteristics have been changed. Dialogue and events have been recreated from memory to convey the substance and essence of what happened but only represent the author's recollection of the events.

Thank you to the many women who read my *Autobiography of an Orgasm* and gave me permission to share their stories.

ONE

There came a point sometime between being fondled by a teenage neighbor when I was six and raped by an acquaintance when I was forty that my body shut down to feeling any pain—or pleasure—until finally, at the age of forty-five, I took myself on as a research project to see if I could feel my orgasm after a lifetime of feeling nothing.

I wrote a book about my sensual research. *Autobiography of an Orgasm* has a big O on the cover. Orgasm is written in small letters across the bottom of the book cover. My mom called it my Oprah book because she jokingly said, "We don't say the O word." And that was the truth. Mom and I had never discussed sex as I was growing up. When the book was released, I was fifty-one and my mother was eighty-one, and we had never had a sex talk.

During the summers when I was a child, most Sundays after church, we would drive twenty-five minutes to my see my maternal grandparents, who lived on a 200-acre farm outside of

Indianapolis. I remember knowing how much was left of my summer vacation based on how tall the corn had grown.

The trips to the farm were mostly filled with silence even though there were seven of us in the car—my parents in the front seat and my four siblings and I spread out in the other seats of the station wagon. Being the second youngest, I'd end up in the way, way back. This was in the late 1960s and early 1970s. I don't remember my parents listening to the radio. I do remember my dad rolling down his window just enough to let fresh air in, and the sound of the wind guided us all the way to the farm and then home. Later I discovered that in other parts of the US, there was a sexual revolution going on in the '60s and '70s, but not in Indiana.

My family had conservative, Christian values. My parents went to church, so I went to church. My parents believed in God, so I believed in God. My parents never talked about sex, so I never talked about sex. On the one occasion I can remember Mom talking to me about the female body, she simply pointed and softly whispered, "Down there," so you can imagine my mother's response when I released *Autobiography of an Orgasm*. She was not thrilled.

The UK's *Sunday Times* called the book a "part erotic, part refreshingly sincere roadmap for the orgasmically challenged . . . sort of an anti-*Fifty Shades of Grey*."

I cringed when I read the review. It was not a life goal to be called orgasmically challenged. The book was a spiritual memoir about my five years of researching orgasm as a way to heal from what experts would label female sexual dysfunction. I would skip the label and claim that really my body was protecting itself from feeling anything after a lifetime of not feeling safe.

A teenage neighbor was the first one to "grab my pussy" when I was six. The next time it happened, I was ten and walking to piano lessons when a group of boys my age started following me. They pushed me into the bushes and lunged at me, three sets of hands poking at my genitals and unformed breasts. When I got home, I told my mom I wanted to quit piano. It happened again at fourteen when a teenage boy stuck his hand inside my panties as I sat next to him in the back seat of the car while his father drove us to a party. At sixteen, the elevator operator at the Indianapolis Athletic Club groped me in the elevator as I was on my way to swim practice. Rather than tell someone about the violation, I quit the swim team. That was not the last time someone "grabbed my pussy" without permission, only the last time it happened before the age of eighteen.

I stayed quiet until my mid-forties when I committed to the research that led to the healing and liberation of my body, my orgasm and my voice.

I was not prepared for what happened after the release of the book. When an excerpt was published in *The Rebelle Society*, an online magazine, one woman suggested I should get therapy and keep it a private matter. After my friend, novelist Dan Wakefield, wrote a review of the book for *NUVO* newspaper in my hometown of Indianapolis, a woman said to Dan at a dinner party, "Betsy's poor mother."

When the book came out, Mom chose not to read it, and I understood why. "We don't talk about those things," she said. I could hear her mother and her grandmother and generations of women in my family—and in your families—saying the same thing: "We don't talk about those things."

Mom modeled for me how to be positive and to think positive. The first time I saw her cry was when my dad died. I was twenty-five and she was fifty-five. If Mom had ever cried before then, she didn't do it in front of me. Like many women, we learned to smile and act like everything was okay.

My birth family stayed quiet after my book was released. There was little or no response from my four siblings. My mom asked a few questions, but mostly we didn't talk about it.

By the time I completed the book, I was healed from the sexual assault I experienced as a child and teenager and from a date rape as an adult. As my body healed, I felt myself coming to life at age fifty, a time when many women are being dismissed by our society. The year before the book release, during an evening out with new friends in Cape Town, South Africa, one of the men joked, "No one wants fifty-year-old pussy" as they spoke about another woman. I laughed along with the group, too ambivalent at the time to speak up, even though I was forty-nine but looked younger. They were unaware of my age. I had finally found my orgasm and felt good in my body and was being told it was too late.

I made the choice to release the book without any reviews. It was unconventional but I wanted the book to be read by women without being influenced by endorsements. I was hoping it would gain an audience through word of mouth. As women read the book, I started receiving stories from all around the world.

I swear you were writing about me. You spoke for me. You allowed me to see myself and appreciate myself in a way I never have.

I share so many of the same experiences as you—it's interesting to hear my story in your story: early abuse by a neighbor, lack of boundaries, abortion, lack of sexual zeal, divorce, lack of emotional and physical feeling, being disconnected from orgasm or faking it.

It's nice to hear my story in someone else's experience. You are brave in all the tiny ways that matter and show me I can be too.

I read your book and then gave it to my husband to read. You opened us to new levels of communication and transparency.

I learned so much from your story and now understand the complexity of a woman to express herself in the world—especially after repeated trauma.

Your book is a testament to the healing power of sensuality, pleasure and truth telling.

Your book helped me start living again.

It wasn't just my story. It was a universal story—at least for the one in three women who experience sexual assault during their lifetime, more than half before the age of eighteen. I received hundreds of emails and had moving conversations with women as I traveled the world teaching writing workshops and retreats. Each story I heard revealed the same message: Once a woman disconnects from her body, she doesn't feel whole. The detachment from her genitals cuts her off from nurturing an area of her body that was meant to express itself.

There was another common theme—almost every one of them stayed silent after experiencing abuse. And if they did speak up, most of the time, they weren't believed, or the blame was put back on them.

Writer and activist Maggie Marie said, "Women who have voices are attacked. Women who are strong are attacked. Women who don't say anything are attacked in the line, "Well, why didn't you come together sooner?" way. You can't win in this game because the cards are stacked against you."

Many women shared stories that were harder to hear:

I wish I had your courage. I think it's too late for me. The damage is too deep.

A friend abused me as a seven-year-old. In college, I was raped. I've kept these secrets for sixty years. I've never enjoyed sex.

One of those letters came from a friend of a friend. Her name was Ella.

Dear Betsy,

Thank you for writing your book. Your courage has encouraged me to start the healing that I know I desperately need after rape in college and disconnection from my body. My mother was raped, too, and she never spoke about it. How do you let go of so much shame? How do you enjoy a body that has brought you so much pain?

—Ella

One of the most horrifying things Ella shared with me (and I'm sharing here with her permission) is that during the rape in college she was cut by the men raping her. They left visible scars all over her body. They told her another man would never want her.

When I met Ella, it was more than ten years after the rape. She was happily married to a wonderful man, and she had just given birth to her second child. She was a gorgeous woman. Her smile and eyes twinkled. We sat chatting as she nursed her newborn with her other son cuddled next to her. She was glowing. Ella had a fulfilling life, and she was thoughtful about nurturing herself as much as she nurtured her children and husband.

"Since the rape in college," she told me, "I have never had sex with my husband without my body being covered. I always leave a t-shirt or top covering my body. I don't want anyone to see the scars."

I know so many women, including myself at one time, who cover themselves due to scars on the inside or outside. Our bodies become a map of the history of our sex life. Our bodies also carry the history of our families and the collective wound of so many of us carrying stories of being assaulted and not speaking up. But Ella had wounds you could see, and she was careful to keep them covered, even from her husband.

I included Ella's letter and my response in *Autobiographies of Our Orgasms, Vol. I, A Collection of Readers Stories* and I'm offering part of my response again here.

Ella,

There is no one solution for everyone. We are all different, so it's really important to listen to your inner wisdom. I know at the start of my orgasm research, when I committed to the thirty days of stroking my clitoris just to feel whatever came up, I really had to pay attention to each stroke, listen to my body's feedback, and make the tiniest adjustments to try and feel even more. It was me becoming the expert on myself. I stopped judging myself and was instead just curious.

How do you get better at listening to your body? One thing that really helped me was taking Qoya classes. I'm not sure where you live, but you can check the website (www.qoya.love) for local classes and retreats and to see if it interests you. There are even free videos on the site. The classes are part dance and part yoga (no levels and no experience required). A Qoya class is designed to help you remember how your body likes to move by paying attention to the feeling in your body. I remember being a kid on the playground and only doing the things I loved during recess because they made me feel good. As a child, I wouldn't repeat a movement over and over again if it didn't feel good in my body. As adults, we shouldn't either. During Qoya class, we spend one song shaking each part of our body. We shake as a way to reset on a cellular level and to move the stuck energy through us. It's using movement as medicine. Qoya was as important to me as the thirty days of stroking my clit to feel my orgasm again because it revealed to me how to listen to my body, and with each class, I feel like I liberate a little more of my authentic self. And the classes made it easier for me to listen to my body when I was doing the more intimate research to feel my orgasm.

I also recommend spending three to four minutes during the morning and at night giving yourself a massage. Put on a favorite song while you do it. I call it the Water Blessing Massage Ritual, because our bodies are over 70% water, and the self-massage is a way to imprint love on each part of your body. Remember when I wrote in Autobiography of an Orgasm about my nearly dead orchid *coming back to life when I told it I loved it daily for thirty days? This massage sends a message of love to your body. Your cells will carry the message through the day or through the night as you sleep. It may sound like a corny thing to do—like telling a plant you love it—and it may be uncomfortable at first. Do it like your life depends on it, though, because it does. Our vaginas and brains are connected, and when we cut off feeling from all the nerve endings in our genitals, we deny our brains the signals that nourish our bodies, stimulate our creativity and give us a sense of wellbeing. Try it for seven days, and then extend it to forty.*

I think many of us had mothers and grandmothers who experienced sexual trauma and never spoke about it or healed from it. Some of our great-great-grandmothers were even burned for it.

When we don't choose to heal, the shame and disillusionment get passed on to the next generation. We have to be braver than our mothers were, because we can't afford to pass this on to our daughters. And we can't afford to live less than fully in our bodies in this lifetime. If we do, we continue the cycle of abuse, except instead of the men who raped us or the boys who assaulted us in college, we become our own abusers by not choosing to heal and recover. It's a choice we make each day when we look in the mirror and see ourselves with love or see ourselves with judgment.

Releasing the shame and enjoying your body after the abuse you experienced requires you to be a tiny bit braver than you have been before. It's a choice. It's worth it. I know you can do it. I did.

—Betsy

About eighteen months after I met Ella, I received a message from her.

"I had sex with my husband fully naked the other night," she wrote. "I know you know what a big deal it was for me."

Ella didn't need to write anymore. I knew it was reclamation. I knew it was her remembering her scars were reminders of the places she had healed.

My scars had been ones you couldn't see, those energetic and emotional wounds under the skin that stay with you because there is nothing to put a Band-Aid on. As I read Ella's words, I remembered my scars were healed too.

I did not know that finally telling my story would be like ripping a Band-Aid off an unhealed wound.

TWO

At the age of thirty-five, I had a life that looked good. I was married with four children I adored. I had a husband that I adored. And I had a secret. I smiled often, even though on the inside I was drowning in tears from not speaking up after sexual abuse and harassment as a child and teenager. I didn't realize those unreleased tears were suffocating me until the rage I should have expressed years earlier became depression, and the judgment about my body and what I'd experienced often left me sick from all the toxic energy I kept inside. On the outside, I stayed positive. I said, "yes, yes, yes" during sex, even though I wasn't feeling a thing. When it came to orgasm, for more than half my life, I was smiling and faking it.

Now, I try to remember the moment everything changed. What was the moment when I was finally unwilling to live among the lies and secrets that became an invisible cage for over forty years? There was the shame of early sexual assault by a teenage neighbor who probably meant no harm; she was just curious, and looking back, I suspect she experienced molestation along the way too. I suspect all of us staying quiet leads to generations of women not living embodied in the truth of their cells.

The first secret led to many more. I thought I could hide from them, and they would disappear as I got older. I didn't realize the cells of my body were holding the story of my life like a good historian taking down notes. My body wouldn't let me forget.

There were three main events that pushed me to try and save myself, to discover who I was beyond the wounds of the past.

One was watching my children become teenagers. When each of them was eleven, I sat them down and told them as much as I could about bodies and sex. My three boys could never look at me during the talks. The kids made jokes about "Mom's sex talk" but I gave it anyway because as they were discovering their bodies. I didn't want them to grow up with the shame I experienced.

The second event was waking up one morning to a letter from my daughter Lucy. She was fifteen, and the letter asked me to find something I loved doing and do it. *Find your bliss*, she wrote. I was making documentary films during this time but could barely show up to edit the films each day. I was thin and fit, but my body was so exhausted from the heaviness of holding secrets. The thing about secrets is you don't realize all the energy that goes into protecting them. Lucy's letter made me want to show up for her as a better example of how a woman stands for herself in the world instead of remaining a silent victim. Rather than thinking about the next film I'd make, at Lucy's urging, I thought about what would make me happy. It took me several years to answer her question.

The third thing that happened—and I've never told anyone this—is at the age of forty-two, I found out I was pregnant. I was living in Miami and seeing a man. I'll call him Dean. He was an artist whose dark personality inspired his brilliant art, but he was not much fun to be around. I slept with him anyway. At the time, I'd been divorced for six years and had had a series of boyfriends, some who were wonderful men, but I couldn't fully let them in. I let them into my body but not into my life. I used my body as a shield for my heart.

With the exception of one of those men, sex was always led by what they wanted in bed and was mostly unsatisfying. I didn't understand that when I was choosing to be intimate with a man, my body was always in a state of shock due to the unhealed and unacknowledged trauma I'd experienced from molestation earlier in life. I didn't know all the secrets I'd kept of the history of assault remained hidden in my body like a shadow, following me as I tried to run away. Even though I felt safe with my boyfriends, my body didn't, so having sex was like exposing a wound over and over again. But Dean's energy was as dark as the part of my past I was trying to hide. I was making the choice to sleep with a man who didn't make me feel safe. I had become my own abuser.

When I suspected I could be pregnant from having sex with Dean, I went alone to the doctor in Miami. I was on the pill but remembered missing two days. While I'd wanted more children, I knew I didn't want a baby with this man. The visit reminded me of going alone to the doctor when I was nineteen and finding out

I was pregnant. My boyfriend at the time gave me the money to have an abortion. I went by myself to end the pregnancy and I carried the judgment and shame of the decision with me for years. But this time I wasn't a young college student; I was a divorced mother of four children.

When I shared the news with Dean, a wave of darkness surged from him. "You bitch, you planned this," he yelled. I was afraid he was going to attack me. I'd never had a man hit me, but I could feel his words punch me. I quickly left and kept the secret of the pregnancy to myself.

Two weeks later, I woke up to blood running down my upper thigh. I returned to the doctor.

"You are miscarrying," she said.

Thank you, I silently whispered to no one. Those words carried the disgrace my body wasn't safe anymore for a soul to be brought into the world and the shame of not willing that spirit to stay with me. That night I was hosting a birthday party for my daughter in our Miami home. I was wearing a large pad in my panties to absorb the blood as I smiled and danced like everything was okay.

A few years later, I received the handwritten letter from my daughter Lucy willing me to live out loud again, to do what she had been brave enough to do—to break the silence and ask me to look for joy.

THREE

"Me too."

"Me too."

"Me too. Me too. Me too. Me too. Me too."

Those were the words that I heard over and over again from women and men who read my book, *Autobiography of an Orgasm.*

"Me too. I was molested as a child and was too scared to tell anyone."

"Me too. I was a sexually curious teenager but felt taken advantage of by teenage boys who played with my body without asking permission."

"Me too. I was raped in college, but because it was someone I knew, I didn't think it was rape, so I stayed quiet."

"Me too. I've been molested by a man, and then he threatened me to stay quiet."

"Me too. I had sex with men, even with my husband, that wasn't satisfying."

"Me too. I didn't think I could have an orgasm. It was easier just to fake it."

"Me too. I thought something was wrong with me, and I was too embarrassed to talk to anyone about it."

"Me too."

It was humbling to find out other women had been staying quiet, too, because telling the truth could mean adding more judgment and shame. Poet and activist Audre Lorde wrote, "Breaking silence is an act of courage and an act of creation."

In my hometown of Indianapolis, except for a handful of supportive friends, people avoided talking to me about the book. Others dismissed it.

"I don't need to read this," one former boyfriend said when I ran into him at a restaurant. "I'd know if a woman was faking it with me."

"You are making too big a deal of this book," a guy I knew said as a way to remind me that what I was doing was insignificant. "People read books and move on."

Women were the opposite. If they hadn't read the book, they would lean in and tell me about their wild sex stories and then recommend their favorite vibrator.

"You'll never have a problem again," a woman told me. "I keep vibrators stashed all over my house."

It was a different conversation with women and men who read the book. I began to receive hundreds of messages from readers telling me about how the book inspired them to finally reveal and release the impact of their own trauma, some from childhood, some current. They finally decided to stand for the wellness and vitality of their sensual and physical bodies. No toys, no plastic, only curiosity for exploring the mysteries of how their bodies were wired to feel ecstasy. Tosha Silver, author of *Outrageous Openness,* wrote to me, "Many will be helped by this book . . . and especially if shame or hatred for your body or sexuality is an issue, it might shift your entire life."

Two of the most meaningful messages came from my own godsisters, Wendy and Cathy, who were now in their late sixties. We'd lost touch after my godmother, Betty, died twenty years earlier. I believe Betty's death was the beginning of the unraveling of my tightly wound life of silence. Wendy and Cathy wrote to me the things that I longed to hear from my own sisters. "I wish I had known," Cathy wrote. "I'm sorry you had to carry that sadness for so long." Later, as Wendy embraced me when I visited her in Maui, I leaned into her hug, never knowing what it was like for my own sisters to hold me in my truth.

I spoke to my four adult children before the book release to explain why it was important to write my story. Two of my boys, Sam and Willie, were comedians who promptly used the book in their stand-up acts, but they also understood the impact of being vulnerable in storytelling. I smiled, remembering the truth of a favorite Nora Ephron quote, "Everything is copy." For someone who was so disconnected from my sexuality for so long, telling the truth about it was a way to take some of the most shameful moments of life and turn them into something that matters. Or, as actress Carrie Fisher reminded us, "Take your broken heart, make it into art."

One former boyfriend did give me permission to write about us in the book. Eli, the lover I wrote about who experienced a fractured penis during sex, gave his blessing to tell the story. "I'm proud of our love story," he wrote to me. I marveled a man could write those words even after experiencing a traumatic injury and emergency surgery after sex with me. I wondered if he would write an endorsement for future lovers who were concerned they might need good medical insurance to date me.

My ex-husband wasn't as understanding as Eli. Ben, the father of my four children, told me he'd sue me if I wrote about our marriage. I reminded him the book wasn't about him or anything he did wrong in our marriage; it was about my own struggles with hiding from the truth of my past. Within a year, he had kicked me out of the house I was living in, which was still in his name, knowing I didn't have savings to get another home.

Several months after the book was published I was visiting Byron Bay, Australia in early 2015, and my friend Mirna invited me to see Elizabeth Gilbert speak. Elizabeth was touring with her best friend Rayya Elias, who wrote a book about surviving drug addiction. After the event, Liz and Rayya were signing copies of their books in the lobby. A line of mostly women waited to meet them. To speed things up, one of their assistants wrote my name on a sticky-note so that Liz and Rayya wouldn't have to ask me if it's Betsy with an -ey or -ie. "Just a -y," I would have replied.

When it was my turn, I congratulated Rayya on her book and asked her how she was brave enough to write stories that might hurt some of the people she wrote about. I explained I had just released a book, and some people close to me were upset that I wrote about them. Before Rayya could answer, Liz took my book to sign it and said, "If they wanted you to write nicer things about them, they should have treated you better." Then, without looking up, she passed the signed books to me, imprinted with her signature and her advice.

Every time a woman quietly shared her story with me, I got a little braver in standing for mine. One night, on the way to speak at an event titled "Censorship and Women's Bodies," I got the urge to call Andy. We hadn't dated for years but as someone who was asking women to speak up, I got the urge to finally ask Andy to apologize for calling me a "cunt" and "whore" while we were dating. Like many trigger words (pussy, cunt, bitch), I don't have a problem with the words now, but it mattered to me that he said them in a derogatory way and that I didn't speak up. What would I want my daughter to do if the same thing happened to her? I pulled my car to the side of the rode and dialed his number. Cars rushed past as I waited for him to answer.

"Hello." He picked up.

"I need you to apologize for calling me cunt and whore," I said. "What?" he said. "Why is this coming up now?"

"Because I just got brave enough to ask you."

Andy apologized. I reminded him that the way he treated any woman impacts his four daughters.

It wasn't as easy speaking up to my former husband. Ben and I had always been decent and respectful towards each other, even thirteen years post-divorce. Our friends and family told us how much they admired the way we remained a family after the end of our marriage. And then my book was released, and everything changed. Ben demanded that I move out of my Indianapolis home. He had given it to me after the divorce so I'd always have a home for our children and eventually grandchildren to share meals and holidays even after they were raised. Ben never put it in my name, and I never asked. It was one of the many times I didn't use my voice. After telling me to vacate the home, he said to me, "I'll continue to support you until you get your shit together."

At the time, I had completed three documentary films and launched an NGO in Zimbabwe to assist at-risk children and endangered animals. I worked as many hours as Ben, but my work was not sustaining me financially. Did that mean I did not "have my shit together?" What was my worth? It felt like my role in my family was being erased.

In her upcoming book, *The Voice Thief,* Gail Schock writes: "Manipulation, gaslighting, isolation, fear led dominance, sexual and mental abuse and financial control are the tip of the domestic violence iceberg. There is more going on underneath than can be identified at any one point, over time it builds to create a wall around you and the truth. *Was it really that bad or not? Did I make this bit up, maybe that was me, I'm sensitive and he is always busy and does so much.'"*

As I moved out quietly a few months later I thought, *Someday you are going to look back on this as one of the best things that ever happened to you.*

My friend Eliana summed it up one night at dinner in London when I was trying to make sense of my ex-husband's anger towards me.

"Well, you told the world he never gave you an orgasm," Elaina exclaimed.

I was silent. I had never thought about it that way.

"That was not my intention," I said defensively. "I never said anything negative about him. If I make anyone look bad, it was me. I was the one not speaking up or asking for what I wanted. I was the one lying."

"None of that makes a difference," she laughed. "He's a man and you bruised his ego."

Should I have stayed quiet so that I didn't offend or hurt or disappoint other people? It made me wonder how many of us don't speak our truth because we fear rejection or financial rape or being abandoned by others. We choose to stay quiet—and then we abandon ourselves.

There are consequences for staying quiet, and there are consequences for speaking up. After a lifetime of staying quiet, I was not prepared to deal with the results of speaking up. By finally using my voice, I was literally left without a home, and it reminded me on a daily basis I had to choose to treat my body as a sanctuary—because it was the only home I had left.

FOUR

In 1953, researcher Alfred Kinsey published *Sexual Behavior in the Human Female,* and in the book he claimed, "The range of variation in the female far exceeds the range of variation in the male."

Apparently this information didn't get to my mother living on a farm in Indiana. "The only thing I knew about sex growing up was what we learned by watching the animals on our family farm," she told me. "There was no talk about the birds and the bees."

The year I was born, 1963, *The Feminine Mystique* was published. The author, Betty Friedan, made the case that women needed to "find" themselves, that women longed for an identity beyond the tradition role of "sexual passivity, male domination and nurturing maternal love" that was a common experience for women at the time. Freidan wrote, "Our culture does not permit women to accept or gratify their basic need to grow and fulfill their potentialities as human beings, a need which is not solely defined by their sexual role."

After the book's release, the seeds were planted for the Women's Liberation movement and women of the 1960s and '70s demanded social, political, and economic freedom.

The liberation didn't end there. There was also a sexual revolution that led to the book *Our Bodies, Ourselves* in 1971. Until then, most women received information about their bodies only from their doctors, who were predominately male. The book, which sold four million copies, offered women information about their bodies, health, and sexuality. It was a call for women to take full ownership of their bodies. It was liberating, but it was not enough.

It's been fifty years since the beginning of the Women's Liberation movement. Today women have access to more information than ever about their bodies and sex. Why then, with all this advancement, are we still accepting that one in five of us has sexual dysfunction? Where is the liberation? I believe that number is closely tied with women not speaking up about sexual assault and not feeling safe in their bodies.

For many years, I was the one in five until I dedicated my time, energy, and attention to something that mattered in my life—discovering my orgasm. Without knowing it, I was retraining my body to feel safe enough to feel pleasure in a world that thought it was okay to "grab my pussy."

There was no one way to get there. Some experts said to focus on the clitoris. Others said to focus on the G spot, which was named after a man, the German gynecologist Ernst Gräfenberg who claimed he discovered it in the 1950s. About three hundred years earlier, in 1559, an Italian surgeon named Realdo Columbo was credited for discovering the clitoris. In the early 1900s, another man, Sigmund Freud, claimed the only real orgasm for a woman was through vaginal penetration. He said experiencing climax only through clitoral stimulation was a sign of sexual immaturity and even labeled those women frigid. Mature women climax only through vaginal sex, said Freud.

While I appreciated their curiosity, I wanted to tell Columbo, Gräfenberg, and Freud to leave the researching and naming of a woman's body to a woman. As Georgia O'Keefe once said, "I feel there is something unexplored about woman that only a woman can explore."

During the sensual research that became my book *Autobiography of an Orgasm*, I observed myself and others search for the next course to take or product to try. Through word of mouth we booked appointments with the current popular yoni massage therapist who specialized in stroking the vulva and vagina as a way to feel, heal and expand our orgasms.

None of those therapists were nearby, so we made investments to travel great distances in pursuit of a great orgasm. We listened to podcasts and books on tape to learn the latest breakthroughs and secrets to good sex. We ordered jade eggs to strengthen our vaginas and dildo-shaped herbal sticks to rebalance our vaginas. In the same way some women get facials, we started to steam our vaginas. We were all looking for the same thing—

how to enhance the feeling in our genitals, how to feel more of our orgasms.

And having one orgasm wasn't enough. We needed to have multiple orgasms and extended orgasms and even extended massive orgasms. In the end, I think what I was looking for was truth and connection, not just to my orgasm, but also to myself. The problem was, I was looking for someone else to give it to me.

After the release of the book, I often received messages from women asking me to recommend a course or yoni therapist. Like me, everyone was searching for that one expert to reveal something or do something to them that would help them experience their first orgasm or the best orgasm ever. I would offer some of my resources, but I always recommended that they follow their own curiosity. There was no right path for healing.

And then one woman wrote to me words that made my heart sink. "I'm glad you found your orgasm," she wrote. "But it's too late for me. I can't afford to take courses like you did, and even if I did; I don't have a partner to experiment with. I'm almost sixty. I'm alone. It's too late for me."

No, it's not too late, I wanted to shout through my response to her. *I want to show you it's possible to feel again at any age. I want you to know that you are the expert on your body. I want you to know that it's possible to experience ecstasy in your body at any age.* Instead, I thanked her for reading the book and for taking the time to write to me. I couldn't offer her anything else because I hadn't already lived it.

For days, I thought about her letter, and then I came up with a solution. I decided to take myself on as a research project again to see what would happen if I lived for a year without having a partner or lover. I wanted to know my body without looking for the answers in a book or finding them in a course in sexuality. I wanted to listen to my body instead of a sex expert. I wanted to know what was possible without relying on a lover to take me there. I was almost fifty-two and committed to a year without sex with a partner so I could speak authentically on how to keep a body turned on. No partners, no toys, no distractions. Just me.

It turned out to be the most sensual year of my life.

FIVE

My idea to not be intimate with anyone for a year seemed like an easy agreement, especially since after my book was released, I stopped getting asked out on dates. Were men intimidated by my honesty? Or was it because they were afraid I would write about them? Maybe it was my age?

"But what happened with the guy you were seeing at the end of the book?" a friend asked. "He sounded promising."

In *Autobiography of an Orgasm*, I took the readers along with me on my first date with Patrick. I met him after completing my five years of researching orgasm that eventually became the book. The book was almost done. Patrick contacted me through Facebook. He was my age and divorced. Our first conversations flowed easily. We had many mutual friends. He even told me he remembered meeting me twenty-five years earlier at a Kenny Loggins concert in Indianapolis. I agreed to go on a date with him even though I didn't remember him or the concert.

We met at a popular Indiana restaurant for our first date. My first feeling when I saw him was he is not for me. It had nothing to do with his looks, he was handsome, it was just the instinct I had in my body. During dinner, Patrick and I had easy conversation. He had a smile like Jack Nicholson, so even if he was saying something I didn't agree with, he pulled me in with his smile. By the end of dinner Patrick moved from sitting across the table to sitting next to me, our bodies touching before our lips did. As we walked outside, Patrick took my hand. The book ends with Patrick and me getting poison ivy after we made out in a nearby grassy field.

"So did you go out again?" my friend asked.

"Yes," I said. "As the rash was healing, a second date happened. He invited me to his house and cooked for me. He poured me glasses of wine and fed me as we shared stories and laughter."

I was finally feeling comfortable in my body after so many years of shame and judgment. I decided to sleep with him that night. And for someone who had just finished writing a book about listening to my body, I was surprised I wasn't able to connect to him during sex. It was disconnected, fast sex like I had just claimed to heal from. I did have an orgasm, I wasn't faking it anymore, but there wasn't any passion or intimacy between us.

I didn't hear from him in the days after. And then it was a week. The poison ivy disappeared, and so did Patrick.

For a few days, I questioned myself for letting him in so quickly (figuratively and literally). I know I can have one or two glasses of wine and still be clear and trust my instincts, but that night Patrick kept my glass full as the food and conversation flowed. I would be more mindful next time. And then I remembered, was I really listening to my body, or had I ignored the signs?

I remember being told to trust my gut when it came to making decisions, but so many times what my gut was telling me was not reasonable, so my mind took over and made another decision.

I'd studied BodyTalk energy medicine with Janet Galipo, intuitive healing with Laura Day, and Mindscape with Kris Attard. These courses helped me expand and trust my ability to listen to intuition and also be able to "read" people.

I also took a Qoya class with Qoya creator, Rochelle Schieck. Qoya is designed around learning to read yourself—to really listen to the truth of your body. After taking that first class, I signed up for Qoya teachers' training as a way to deepen my understanding of the messages my body had been sending my whole life but that I had neglected.

For years, I'd ignored the tightness in my stomach when something didn't feel right. I kept quiet about the things that mattered to me because it felt too risky to speak up. My study of BodyTalk, Mindscape, Qoya, and other modalities confirmed what I always knew—that my body was constantly sending me messages. I was thinking my way through life, and Qoya invited me to feel my way. At first I couldn't feel a thing, but the more I danced with the movement of the class, the more I began to listen and integrate my body into my decision-making.

I wasn't spiritual, but I started considering that something else might be in charge instead of my mind. I noticed that whenever I was supposed to pay attention to something, I'd get a "hit" in my body. Sometimes it was a zing up my spine, sometimes it was a full-body tingle, and sometimes it was an inhalation deeper than normal. Even if I didn't have the bigger picture, I paid attention to those moments and stored whatever was going on around me for later.

With my orgasm research, I appreciated the wisdom of the experts, but the change for me came when I started listening less to the teachers and more to the instincts of my body. After years of believing that sex needed to be hard and fast, my body was asking me to slow down so I could listen deeply. I was surprised that I could feel more when sex was slower.

The first day of my research started the morning after I made the decision to not be with anyone for a year. I've always been a morning person. As a teenager, I was up by 5:00 a.m. for early-morning swim practices before school. In college, I'd go for a run before classes. With lovers, I preferred sex in the morning when our bodies were rested and relaxed. It felt good to wake up to the soft strokes of a boyfriend's touch after sleeping next to him all night. With the research, I would be waking up alone for the next 365 days.

I woke up in the bed of my Indiana home, the one I'd be vacating soon. My kids were all away, living in four different states. The house was quiet. I checked the clock. It was 7:33 a.m. How much time was I going to dedicate to this daily research? I hadn't decided. I easily made time for thirty-minute manicures or sixty-minute blow dry appointments for my hair. I should spend as much time cultivating my sensual energy as I did on a pedicure, right? Forty-five minutes sounded good. Over a year that would be committing to over 264 hours of mindfully tending to my sensual body. I remembered in the book *Outliers*, Malcolm Gladwell wrote it takes 10,000 hours to master something. At this rate it would take me another forty years to master my orgasm.

My hand drifted under the covers and cupped my genitals. I took ten long deep breaths to connect and listen.

"Listen to your pussy," a woman once told me.

What?! I thought at the time. *What does my vagina sound like? Does she have a sassy accent like Mae West or does she purr like Eartha Kitt?*

It was quiet in the room, so I listened.

Nothing. My vagina was silent.

I decided to begin with a self-massage starting at my hips. I used both hands to massage one hip and then the other. My skin tingled as I gently rubbed looking for the place in my touch that felt good. My back instinctively arched as my hands traveled to the inside of my thighs. As I caressed each thigh, my breath got heavier and I could feel the crest of a wave of euphoria wash under and over my skin. Each inhale delivered an intoxicating elixir that seemed to make the area beyond my skin expand and vibrate. The exhales shot electric currents throughout my body like lightening hitting the ground and then electrifying the landscape.

The fingers on my right hand grazed the outer lips of my vulva, and suddenly my vagina was pulsing.

I pulled my hand away and tried to use my breath to slow down my climax, but it was too late. After so many years of denying my orgasm as a way to not feel pleasure or pain, my body was now willing to release a surge of bliss. I sighed as ecstasy flooded the cells that held the secret code of my inner world.

I checked the clock. It was 7:58 a.m. I'd already climaxed, and I still had twenty more minutes of research. I decided to save it for later that day.

That night as I went to bed, I pressed shuffle on the music library on my cell phone. Seal's song "Kiss from a Rose" came on. I smiled, thinking about the first time a man played that song for me. His name was Alex. We were in a hotel room in Paris and had spent a long day walking the city. Since he was French, I saw Paris through the eyes of my lover. Alex spoke enough English and I spoke enough French, but we still couldn't fully communicate everything we were feeling because of the language barrier. We wanted to see a play together, and I smiled at his brilliant choice of *Stomp*—part dance and part percussion—a unique musical that didn't need words. We both enjoyed it.

Back at the hotel room, Alex prepared a bath for us. I got in first, letting the hot water warm my skin after the walk home in the cool evening rain. Alex gave me privacy in the bathroom. I sank deeper into the tub, extending my legs until my toes touched the far edge. What was I doing there? My four young children were back in the US with their father. We had agreed to split, but I still didn't feel like I could fully be with another man. Suddenly, tears ran down my cheeks. I held my breath and put my head under the water, letting my tears mix with the bubbles. I loved the silence under the water. I was on the swim team when I was younger, and I always loved the moment of diving in and everything becoming peaceful. I'm sure it had something to do with feeling safe in the water. I was a strong swimmer; no one could get to me in the pool.

When my head rose above the surface of the bath, I heard Seal's voice singing "Kiss from a Rose." The door to the bathroom opened, and Alex was standing naked. I smiled. As beautiful as his body was, my eyes traveled to his eyes. His gaze was so gentle. I started to make space for him and even considered getting out. I'd never shared a tub with a man before. He got in behind me so his legs wrapped around me. I settled into his chest, letting the curve of his body and the lightness of the water hold me. More tears. I was glad I was facing away from him. I wasn't ready to fully reveal myself.

My back touched his chest so I could feel his breath rise and fall. We stayed still for a long time until he reached for the soap and began to wash my back. He gently stroked my shoulders, and then his hands reached around and embraced my neck with soft, gentle strokes. His soapy hands travelled down my front and began massaging my breasts and belly as his hands left trails of bubbles with each area he washed. My body sank into his touch.

His hands moved to my inner thighs, and I closed my eyes as he used the soap and his fingertips to explore. I sighed as his movements moved closer to my vulva. My body instinctively began to stiffen, and my heart started racing. I opened my eyes. I had gone from feeling safe and turned on to feeling anxious. I couldn't help the response. Later I would find out it was my body going into a fight-or-flight mode to protect itself from perceived danger—even though I was safe. The effects of the trauma still lived within my cells from unhealed sexual assault earlier in life. I thought that by ignoring the damage, I could move on and forget it, but my body still remembered.

I turned around in the bath and kissed Alex and told him I was getting out. I wrapped myself in a towel and left the bathroom, restarting the Seal CD before I crawled into bed. Alex stayed in the bath longer. By the time he joined me in bed, the entire album was finished. I kept my eyes closed and didn't move. I could feel his warm skin swaddling my body. I knew I was safe with him; *please let my body calm down.* My heart was still beating rapidly, and my breath was shallow. My heart wanted to make love to him, but my body was still panicked. He put his arms around me, and we fell asleep.

Back in my bedroom in Indiana—alone—it was the end of day one of my commitment to a year of sensual research. I decided to call them my bliss sessions since in her letter to me my daughter Lucy had urged me to find my bliss. I'm sure, however, that this was not what she was expecting.

SIX

I'd never accepted a religious doctrine, especially after finding there was no space for the feminine in religions. Christianity, Hinduism, Islam, and Buddhism were exclusive men's clubs in hierarchy. Men made the rules even though each one of those men was created in the womb of a woman. Could the years of patriarchy have prevented women from remembering the garden we are to return to is under our skin in the place of darkness where creation begins? Maybe the religion we should seek was connected to the place of creation, the womb.

It had only been a month, but I noticed I was walking around with a greater awareness, or maybe the right world was aliveness. My 52nd birthday was in a few weeks and I was feeling more alive than ever. Was it really the daily bliss sessions, or was it Byron Bay, Australia? Maybe it was both.

I arrived in Byron Bay, a coastal beach town on the east coast of Australia a few weeks before my birthday. My friend Mirna lived in Bryon Bay, and I decided it would be the perfect place to launch my 52nd year. Before I left for Australia, I met with Ben who promised nothing would be moved from my house without my permission. I asked him to let me know when it sold so that I could return and finish packing my things.

Australia was a place I'd wanted to return to since I spent a month backpacking through New Zealand and Australia when I was twenty-five. Byron Bay was a beautiful surfing community where I was told there were seven women to every one man. The odds didn't bother me since I wouldn't be searching for a partner during my year of research.

"So you're going to be celibate?" my new friend Deb asked in her Australian accent. "I know so many women abstaining from sex right now."

"Not exactly," I said. "I'm choosing to not have sex with a partner. I'm using the year to deepen my understanding of my own body without the distraction of anyone else. I call them my bliss sessions."

"Abstaining from sex is the next 'in' thing," Deb laughed. "Celibate is the new black."

"But I'm not abstaining from it," I said. "I'm experiencing self-intimacy daily. I'm not giving up my sensual life. I'm actually more turned on than ever."

After just a month of my bliss sessions, I was finding a shift in my perception of sex and how it was represented in our culture. I wasn't having the sex depicted in movies or porn or romance novels. I wasn't even having the sex I'd experienced with my most favorite partners. My bliss sessions were taking me into a new meaning of sex and sensuality where it was not just my birthright to feel good in my body—it was also my responsibility to nourish it in the same way you would water a plant. By deeply listening to my body, the sessions were turning into a form of prayer. For the first time, I was devoted to myself.

I used to wake up and go for walks or runs in the morning. Now, my hand automatically went under the sheet, even if I was barely awake; my body already knew what it wanted and guided me. I scanned my body for any areas that felt good or wanted attention. Instead of the old paradigm of paying attention to what ached in my body, I was searching for the places where a subtle spirit was urging me to explore. Sometimes it was in my genitals, and sometimes it was somewhere else. Often I found myself giving my neck a gentle massage as part of my bliss sessions, tracing circles around my throat with a touch that was light enough to make my fingertips feel like feathers. As I began spending more time caressing my neck, I noticed my pelvic area would flood with tingling sensations and my hips would relax and loosen. Was there a connection between the energy in our throats and the energy in our pelvises?

I felt throbbing around my vulva. Without my thinking about it, my right hand moved to my genitals, and my fingers began circling the outer lips. My moves were guided by the longing of my body. I inhaled deeply and sighed as I traced slow circles. The inside of my vagina contracted. The thumb and middle finger of my right hand began rubbing my clit, not on it but the area around it, gently massaging until I was already feeling the peak of an orgasm. It used to take me twenty, thirty or forty minutes to climax. Now after only a few minutes, I took a deep breath and received waves of ecstasy sending tingling sensations up and down my spine. The sensations continued until I pressed down firmly on my genitals to bring me down from the high. I lay still in gratitude until my breathing went back to normal, remembering in my previous research the importance of resting and restoring so the body has time to recalibrate and store the information. This must be what it's like to worship. You take time to pray and then give thanks.

The food I was eating in Byron Bay was mostly green and mostly grown within a few miles of where I slept. My thoughts were clear and calm. My body was relaxed. It's said that hummingbirds know to go only to the flowers that are sweet. By nurturing my sensual energy, I was finding the sweetness over and over again. Before, I had paid for things that made me happy—a new purse, shoes, and things for my home. Now I found contentment by just appreciating my first home, my body.

In Byron Bay, I experienced sovereignty and an empowerment as I opened myself to live out in the world instead of being confined by a home or even by the label of being a mother or ex-wife. For someone who at one time was clinically labeled with female sexual dysfunction, now I was experiencing a range of orgasm and climax. As long as I didn't rush it, and I let my body guide me, I was having orgasms that were sometimes clitoral, sometimes vaginal, sometimes both. I was also having consciousness-expanding experiences that went beyond the definitions of orgasm, where my body flowed into a state of ecstasy that blurred the edges of my physical body, like I was floating between two worlds. On these days, I noticed that my creativity flowed, and I wrote with ease, never experiencing a lack of words or purpose as a writer.

I'd take long walks at sunset and watch the surfers catching wave after wave. Maybe surfing was their way of living beyond boundaries as they trusted and used their instinct to be carried away.

For my 52nd birthday, Mirna took me to see the play *Vagina Monologues*. It was playing to a sold-out crowd at a nearby theater. I remember being both thrilled and shocked watching the play for the first time. Why had I never seen it before?

In all my years of hiding my secrets and shame, I don't think I was ready for *Vagina Monologues,* but when I finally watched it with Mirna in February of 2015, I laughed, cried and cheered with a crowd of three hundred men and women. Hearing women speak stories out loud instead of hiding from them made me feel a little braver about sharing my own story. At one point, Zen Virago, the MC for the event, asked anyone to stand who had experienced sexual assault or knew someone who had. Nearly everyone stood, including me.

The next day, February 14th, was the annual V Day event of the One Billion Rising celebration, created by *Vagina Monologues* author, Eve Ensler, as a way to remember the one in three women who experience sexual abuse in their lifetime. Byron Bay was known for having one of the largest V Day events in the world. I woke up early, before 6:00 a.m., put on a red kimono, and walked five minutes to the beach. As I walked, I noticed other women in red heading towards the V Day event. Two hundred of us gathered and danced. As the sun was rising, so were we. At the end of the dance, I took off all my clothes and ran into the ocean with many of the other women, letting my body be seen and set free at the same time.

SEVEN

After two months of bliss sessions, I was discovering nuances about my body that I never noticed with a partner. One thing that was important to me during this time was not using any toys, like vibrators or dildos, to stimulate the clit or G spot or cervix. While I didn't have a problem with someone else using toys, my body was craving human touch, not plastic or glass or crystal dildos. I knew that the clitoris and anus (and penis in men) have the highest concentration of nerve endings in the body. The clit has more than 8,000 nerve endings, twice as many as the penis. Our fingers also have a high concentration of nerve endings. By using my own hands instead of a toy, I was allowing myself to receive the most amount of stimulus possible.

When I was first discovering my orgasm, I did use a vibrator, and I always came hard and fast, much like a man. It was a quick release and a quick recovery, and it always felt the same, like a jolt. There was no comparison to what I was experiencing with my own touch. With my bliss sessions, my body was taking me for a ride that was never the same, and each orgasm was more expansive than the last one. I went from having quick climaxes to experiencing my body in an orgasmic state for an hour or more. It reminded me of something Julia Child said,

"I was thirty-two when I started cooking; up until then, I just ate. The measure of achievement is not winning awards. It's doing something that you appreciate, something you believe is worthwhile. I think of my strawberry soufflé. I did that at least twenty-eight times before I finally conquered it."

Before I was just having sex; now I was conquering my erotic energy. I was inviting myself into the darkness and mysteries of my feminine power. The place where I had given birth to life was now suddenly giving birth to me.

EIGHT

It was now time to go back to the US. As much as I loved Byron Bay, I couldn't afford to stay there longer, and I had committed to taking the Qoya Intensive Training for Teachers in March in Costa Rica.

I left sunny Australia and flew back to Indiana. When I'd left my home in January of 2015, there was still a bed, kitchen furniture, a dining room table and a treasured Steinway piano that was given to me by my godparents. I never expected to stay in the house again, but it sat unsold, not even on the market, so I emailed Ben that I planned on staying there with our daughter, Lucy during a brief visit to Indiana in February. Even though I sent three emails to Ben with the information on my dates to stay in the home, he answered none of them. Once again, after so many years of a good divorce, it was sad to see this change in him.

I returned to my Indiana home on a cold, colorless Saturday in February. The day before we were to arrive to stay in my home, Ben sent our daughter Lucy—not me—a text to say that we couldn't stay there. "Get a hotel room," he wrote her. We drove to the house anyway.

Lucy stood next to me, both of us shivering from the below-freezing temperatures as I pressed the code to open the garage door. The door slowly opened to reveal stacks of boxes marked with my name and the names of our children piled high in the garage. It appeared the house had been emptied without my permission. I walked into the kitchen, and everything except the kitchen table was gone, including a treasured orchid, now frozen on the floor in the garage.

I walked to my rental car. I wanted to be "okay" for my daughter. Would I model to my twenty-five-year-old daughter that it's okay to be emotionally raped by her father? I took a deep inhale of the chilly winter air and smiled at her. "I'm good," I said. "We'll stay somewhere else."

Years earlier, the night our divorce agreement was finalized, Ben and I went out to eat because it was a Tuesday night and for years we had Tuesday night dates. That night he held my hand and said, "I will always take care of you." Even though the marriage didn't last, I felt we had a mutual desire to support each other as parents.

After the divorce, I moved with the children to Miami and he became engaged to Cheryl, a women that was twenty years younger than him. Even as he was engaged to Cheryl, he bought me a home in Indianapolis "so you and the kids will always have a place to live here." He didn't marry Cheryl. Several years later we were surprised to discover he had a secret. Ben was dating Annie who had been our nanny for fifteen years.

During this time, I was healing my own wounds around a lifetime of abuse, first from being molested when I was a child and teenager and continuing into my mid-forties until I finally began to treat my body with love and kindness instead of judgment and hate for everything that happened to me. Ben never knew of any of this part of my history and I wandered if our relationship could have been saved, if I'd been brave enough to share it with him during the marriage.

The house being packed without my permission felt like a violation.

Should I stay and fight for the house and for my worth as the matriarch of my family? It was month three of my year of bliss sessions. I listened to my body and trusted when it guided me to walk away.

NINE

I took my first Qoya class with its creator Rochelle Schieck in 2011 at a retreat in Costa Rica. I thought I was showing up for a week of exercise classes and massages. I had no idea. That first class changed my life—it really helped me remember who I was beyond the years of conditioning and stories stuck in my body.

I almost didn't make it through the class. I was instantly triggered by a woman I didn't know (she later became someone I adored) who began to cry early during class. I looked at Rochelle, concerned that this woman was ruining the class. Rochelle continued teaching as the woman lay on her back, sobbing on the studio floor. The rest of us followed Rochelle's lead as she continued to guide us through a yoga sequence. Being a martyr, I thought I needed to save this woman, but since I didn't know her, I kept moving and noticed that no one else tried to "save" her either. No one was trying to fix her.

After two more songs with Rochelle guiding us through a shaking sequence where we shook through every part of our bodies, the woman stopped crying and re-joined the class, even though she never really left it. It was a good example of giving a woman permission to feel what she is feeling and not trying to fix her. By letting her be authentic in the moment, she fixed herself.

I spent a lifetime with a smile on my face, not fully revealing myself. In my family, tears meant you were depressed, and anger, like my dad carried after growing up in a family with an abusive, alcoholic father, meant you were mentally ill. There were consequences for showing either, so I chose to be "normal" and to not reveal myself.

After I lost a baby midway through pregnancy, Ben used to say to me, "You're depressed; take Prozac." Every night, as I took the pill, I remember a tightness gripping my throat and diaphragm. Along with the Prozac, I swallowed shame for thinking there was something wrong with me. The judgment was heavy, like a large boulder lodged against my chest. After weeks of taking Prozac, the tightness disappeared, but it wasn't replaced with anything except a blank feeling, a nothingness that made it easier to smile again and pretend I was okay.

Towards the end of that first Qoya class, I felt a darkness begin to wash over my body. It was a sadness that I had previously ignored. I avoided feeling grief because it meant something was "wrong" with me.

The next dance was a free dance. The song had a quick tempo; one that I thought needed a quick step too. I knew I couldn't dance with the heaviness creeping into every cell. In moments like this, I would retreat to bed, making my room as dark as possible to match my mood. After the music began, I looked around the room and noticed thirty women dancing like they were at a wedding or nightclub. They all seemed to be in a blissful zone. I walked over to Rochelle and quietly said, "I'm going to sit this one out. I'm going through a rough time in my life. I'm experiencing a lot of sadness." And Rochelle said something that changed my life: "Dance from where you are," she said. "Dance with your sadness."

My body took on the invitation before my mind could talk me out of it. My shoulders hunched inward, my chest was tight; my steps were slow like I was in quicksand. I took on my sadness as a dance partner. I didn't cry. I moved. Each inhale became deeper, and each exhale released invisible bubbles of old stories and pain lodged in my breath. In the moment, I'd like to think I lost myself, but really, I found myself in my breath and in my movement. I was honoring my grief by symbolically dancing with it. By the end of the song, the slightest smile was on my face; my shoulders rolled back as my hips and legs circled and swayed around the room. Within three minutes, my dance with sadness became a dance of grace and allowance. The movement became the medicine. And for the first time in a long time, the five year old who loved to sashay around the living room was back.

After that first class, I signed up for the Qoya Teacher Training. The training was offered during the week of the retreat. I had no intention of teaching Qoya; I only wanted to understand the practice so I could continue to do it on my own. It was a practice that made me feel more awake, more like myself. By the end of the week, with my body and spirit liberated, I left Costa Rica with a sense of freedom not from anyone else, but from myself. I had set myself free.

Life at home started to change too. I noticed the benefits from Qoya caused me to eliminate other things in my life. I stopped running and intense yoga workouts. My body still craved cardio and working up a sweat but in softer workouts. I ended some friendships that were unhealthy. How did I know they were unhealthy? I was reminded of the Maya Angelou quote: "...people will forget what you said, people will forget what you did, but people will never forget how you made them feel." It didn't feel good to be around them. My daily routine included doing more of the things that felt good and less of the things that didn't feel good. It was that simple.

I noticed I gradually stopped going to therapy as much. I was working things out—or feeling things out—during Qoya and by being more mindful. My body craved more greens, more water, and more things that matched my vibrant energy.

One of the best things that happened was my increased intuition. In Qoya, we are asked to listen to our body. It's the same as trusting your gut. I was good at listening to my body in a Qoya class and responding with an authentic movement. It didn't stop once I left the class. I made better decisions through the remembering that came with moving my body as my portal to the answers I had previously looked to others to give me.

In March of 2015, three months into my year of bliss sessions, I returned to that same studio in Costa Rica to take the highest level of training for teachers—the Qoya Intensive. Just as I was leaving on the Intensive, I got a call from my son Willie, who had been having a tough year at college after the death of his roommate. I asked him to join me in Costa Rica for a week of surfing and nurturing his body. We flew together to Costa Rica and then shared a shuttle from the airport to the resort, about a three-hour drive. One of the women in the van was also going to the Intensive. Her name was Lindsay, and I told her she looked like my mom's side of the family. "You could be my cousin," I said. Lindsay chatted with Willie about his life, not knowing he was going through some major struggles. Lindsay shared that she had left her two boys—Patrick, age eight and Logan, age four—at home with her husband so she could attend the Intensive. "If I miss my boys and want to give them a hug, I'll come and give Willie a hug instead," she said. When we arrived at the resort that would become our home for the week, Willie turned on the AC full blast and went to bed. I was hoping the energy of the jungle would help him heal.

I was unaware that Willie was using harder drugs to try and numb the pain of his own grief. The clean food and no alcohol or smoking had put his body into a detox, and I noticed he got jitterier every day. I didn't realize it was a smoke-free property, and Willie got in trouble for smoking cigarettes. After four days, he made the choice to return to the US. I hugged him as he left, trusting that he knew what was best for his body but also asking him to speak up if he needed more help.

The rest of the week I gave my attention to the Intensive while most of me was still with Willie. Our days were ten hours long as Rochelle guided sixteen of us through becoming the first fully certified Qoya teachers. The last night during our final ceremony, I walked in the darkness with two of the women, Kaci and Stephanie, to a labyrinth we had built earlier in the day near the beach. The only thing lighting the pathway from the Qoya studio to the beach was the stars. We were to walk the labyrinth one by one as a way to invite ourselves to look inward for the answers. I asked for healing and guidance for Willie and for my family. I didn't get an answer. I walked back to my room in the darkness.

TEN

During the week in Costa Rica, I was unable to do my bliss sessions since I was sharing a room with my son. Even after Willie left, I continued to skip the sessions. It may have been the long days during the Intensive; it may have been the concern for my son's wellbeing. What was I doing dancing in the jungle? Should I have escorted him back to Indiana? I had no home there anymore. Ben said he would pick Willie up from the airport. It made me wonder how it must have felt for a child to be going back and forth between two parents during a divorce. Willie was twenty-two, and he lived in a world where there were no models for men to express their suffering. I had found Qoya and a way to honor my pain and suffering. Willie had found drugs.

When I landed back in Indiana a few weeks later, I had nowhere to stay. My plan was to get a hotel room. There were offers to stay with friends, but I wanted solitude, so I drove to my old home. Since Ben had a new baby, I guessed that nothing had been done with the house. Even though he said he was in a rush to sell it, I suspected nothing had happened in the eight weeks since I had been gone. I was right. The code to get in was still the same. All of the boxes were still piled high in the garage.

When I went inside the home, I found there was a mattress on the floor of my bedroom, and my kitchen table where I wrote was still inside the house. The only other possession left was the Steinway piano given to me after my godfather, Bill, died. The piano was gorgeous and over fifty years old. Ben had encouraged me to sell it but there was no way I was going to let it go.

I went back to the garage and found a bag with my sheets, comforter, and oversized pillows that had been packed without my permission. I brought the bags into the house and made my bed. The master bathroom cabinets still contained my toiletries, and I was surprised to discover my closet hadn't been packed. I lit some candles around my bath, turned on the water, and poured oils into the bath. I guess I was becoming a squatter in my own home.

The next day I woke up to the empty house. Before I was fully awake, my hands instinctively moved down my body and started stroking my inner thighs. My body was remembering my commitment even when my mind would forget. One hand moved to my vagina, dipping a finger inside. It was moist and silky. I inserted my middle finger up to the first knuckle and gently tapped inside, slowly going counterclockwise, feeling the wall of my vagina tense and then release. I used to not feel a thing when I had a finger or a man's penis inside me. My vagina was numb before I took the time to heal. Now I felt along every edge, noticing any sensations that came up in the different parts of my vagina. I inserted my finger a little farther, up to my second knuckle and did the same thing, lightly putting pressure in each area as I made my way around the middle part of my vagina. I knew vaginas were about three to four inches long. It amazed me that it could expand to hold a penis, and during birth it would expand up to 200 percent to allow a baby to pass through. I stuck my finger as far as it would go, up to the last knuckle. My cervix felt soft yet firm. The center of the cervix was tightly shut. I wanted to high-five it for being so discerning to the billions of sperm that tried passing through during my lifetime. I wanted to thank it for allowing in the sperm that fertilized the eggs that eventually became my four children—Sam, Lucy, Willie, and Charlie. Giving birth to each of them were some of the happiest days of my life.

I slowly pulled my finger from my vagina, not feeling the need to explore my orgasm further. I spent a few minutes resting my hands on my belly over my womb, wondering how it knew to provide the nutrients and safe space to grow a baby. Suddenly, I heard a knocking against the bedroom window. I remained still, knowing they couldn't see in because I had the blackout shades pulled down. More knocking, but it didn't sound like a human—it seemed like something was being thrown at the window. I got up, wrapped a towel around me and walked over to lift the shade just as a large cardinal took aim and flew into the window. He knocked himself down when he hit the glass and then jumped up to the railing across from the window and tried again. I opened the shade, thinking he was seeing a reflection and attacking what he thought was another bird. The cardinal dove at the window again. I'd lived in the house for eight years, and this had never happened before.

I went to breakfast and then came back to the house to work on my next book. I loved working at my kitchen table that had an oversized sofa on one side. Windows surrounded the view, so as I wrote I could gaze at the lake I used to live on.

I was working on an anthology of readers' stories. After releasing *Autobiography of an Orgasm*, I began to receive messages from readers who thanked me for writing the book. Every time I read one of the personal stories that a reader shared, I was in awe of her courage to finally reveal something she had hidden for years. She was me. I was her. We were not going to stay silent anymore.

I decided to ask for submissions and selected sixteen stories to create the next book, *Autobiographies of Our Orgasms, A Collection of Readers' Stories.* (As of 2017, three anthologies have been released with over thirty stories. It's like a *Chicken Soup for the Soul* but for orgasm.) I received stories that went beyond the physical to the emotional and spiritual experiences of being a woman. I was also including two stories from men, one who wrote poignantly about how porn negatively affected his intimacy with women.

One of the stories, by Susan Motheral, was about being diagnosed with breast cancer and discovering that the moment she felt like her body was betraying her was actually when she needed to stand for self-love and self-care. A scene she wrote about revealing her post-surgery scars to a group of other women with breast cancer brought tears to my eyes as one by one, they revealed their scars—the places they had healed—to each other.

Another woman wrote about being raped by a trusted guru and the consequences for speaking up in a community that was protecting him. My friend, Tara Dixon, wrote a beautiful story about experiencing an orgasmic birth as she gave birth to her son. These were conversations around sensuality and sexuality that I'd never seen.

Writer S.L. Sourwine wrote a moving piece about making the choice to take her own virginity. In a world that tells girls and women our virginity is something to be "lost" to someone else, S.L.'s choice was a radical act of ownership and sovereignty over her teenage body. I wish I'd had these stories to read when I was a teenager and already feeling shame around my body, or as a grown women and still not understanding that my body—and my ability to orgasm—was not dysfunctional. My body simply didn't feel safe in a world that forgets that all bodies are sacred and to be treated with loving care.

The back and forth communication with each writer was another layer being healed. Maggie Marie Genthner, who wrote a powerful story for the book titled "In The Body of the Goddess" said to me: "I think change is happening. I feel it. We have crossed the point of no return— the scales have tipped in favor of pointing out the predators and unchaining the girls who were told they were liars or crazy. The Buddha said, "There are three things that can't be hidden for long, the sun, the moon and the truth."

A few of the writers chose to publish under pseudonyms because of concerns about judgment from family or former partners or how it might affect their careers. I was experiencing how the choice to speak up had affected my own life, but I was also unwilling to ignore and abandon my body and my truth anymore. It felt like I finally was living from a place of wholeness where my mind, spirit, and body were integrated. The wellness and vitality of my vagina was also connected to the wellness and vitality of my brain and my heart.

My daughter Lucy sent me an excerpt from the book *Men Explain Things to Me* by Rebecca Solnit. Lucy highlighted a passage where Solnit writes about the consequences of women who don't tell their stories and risk being erased.

I sat in the house that I'd been kicked out of and edited the stories of women who were not letting themselves disappear. Through their words they showed me the tremendous ability of the human spirit to alchemize pain and disillusionment into the realization of a sacred body that goes beyond what we see or know. Reading their words showed me how to continue to liberate my life force through using my voice.

ELEVEN

I stayed in Indiana for two months, living in my old home with just the bed and the kitchen table and the Steinway piano. I enjoyed having so much open space in the house. There was no furniture in the living room, just the piano. It was the perfect place to dance in between editing the book. I stayed long enough to get the anthology published. Every day I woke up to the cardinal hitting the window over and over again. I tried soaping the window, taping cardboard to it, but nothing worked. The cardinal was my godmother Betty's favorite bird, and I knew it was a sign to go.

Before I left, I did a book reading with several of the women featured in the anthology. Inspired by seeing *Vagina Monologues* earlier in the year in Byron Bay, I decided to do a spoken-word event in Indianapolis, my birthplace that I'd been running from my whole life. There would be four of us reading our stories: Jeanne Mayhue, Marilene Isaacs Kauffman, Tara Dixon, and myself. Novelist Dan Wakefield, now in his eighties, agreed to host the event. The book reading would be at one of my favorite shops in Indianapolis, The Playful Soul. Maybe thirty people showed up, including my son Sam and his partner Pauline, my daughter Lucy, and my mom. It meant a lot to me to have two of my four children and my mother there. We'd had limited conversations about the book, so the reading would be enlightening to them. It would also be the first time they heard me tell my story out loud.

Dan introduced me, citing our previous work together when I produced a documentary of his book, *New York in the Fifties*, which was released in 2001. I appreciated Dan's support. He'd known me for twenty-five years as a filmmaker, and now he was supporting my voice as a writer—and one who was writing about something provocative. As we read our stories one by one, the air in the room grew thick with the darkness of our tales. Dan had made the audience laugh with his introduction, but there was no laughter during our storytelling. Only Tara's reading was a bit lighter as she described her experience of delivering her first child while her husband was trying to make it home from a business trip.

Tara spoke:

"From my hospital bed I could see a sliver of the city. By some chance the view was directly aligned with the Chrysler Building. I looked at this iconic structure for inspiration as my friend fed me ice chips and my cervix dilated. During the contractions, I counted the art deco triangles and imagined drawing the building in my mind. When I was offered the epidural, I refused it. I wanted my whole body to be present for this experience.

"PUSH!" my doctor shouted. One triangle. Two triangles. Three triangles. Four triangles . . . I would never be able to look at the Chrysler Building in the same way.

"He's crowning!" I remember hearing. We had found out the sex of our baby but had kept it a secret. He even had been named for several months. This was the big moment, and his father was probably somewhere over New Jersey. I had long since left my human existence. I remember wailing and groaning, connecting to my animal-self. Something wondrous happened as I felt this body exiting my vaginal canal. My wailing began to harmonize into music. This music took the form of exhalations of sound that were reminiscent of opera. My whole body was pulsing and throbbing like a musical instrument. A sweet rush of ecstasy emanated from my clitoris. I felt tingling in my mouth, fingers and toes. I continued to sing as my body did the same. This full-body smile faded in slow motion as my son was brought to my chest.

It was recorded that he came out of me at 8:22 am. His father remembers looking at his watch as the plane made contact at exactly the same time. Somehow this synchronicity and the orgasmic bliss made everything all right. No matter who was present and where it took place, a new life had begun, and he came in with a song."

Marilene Isaacs Kauffman, a longtime Indiana resident and well known intuitive, shared a story titled "I Was Born Orgasmic" about her memory of her birth as well as her experience of a kundalini awakening. She read, *"After my son was born, I started to fully drop into my body again and to feel safe. One day when Merlin was about eighteen months old, I was in a grocery store with my husband and him. I suddenly came to an abrupt stop and leaned on the grocery cart as a full body kundalini experience manifested. The switch had been turned back on. I had awakened to the memory of the divine alchemical marriage with the inner beloved, where we live in a constant state of union and orgasm. The cosmos' kundalini energy was back."* The audience was captivated by her storytelling.

The room and our hearts went silent as Jeanne Mayhue read her piece, *"A Women's Voice,"* about the abuse she experienced during her marriage and the moment she got strong enough to walk away. Jeanne stood poised like a ballerina and spoke slowly as she read her story. *"In times prior I would have begged him to forgive me, to calm down, to please, please stay and not be angry. There would have been storming about and something broken, a cut or bruises somewhere on my body from having been in the path of the storm. But not this time. I turned my back to him, braced myself for what might come and tried to dance again."*

After Jeanne read, I could feel the heaviness in the room not because the audience didn't value the stories but maybe because we had never made time to listen to the shadow and honor the voice of a woman's true experience in a world that asks us to smile and fake it. People in the room seemed quiet and speechless, almost hesitant to clap after each speaker.

I looked at Lucy, Sam, Pauline, and Mom sitting near the back. I took a deep breath and started to read. I was surprised to feel my throat tighten and my voice get small. *I have healed from this,* I thought. *Why do I feel tears coming?*

My story was called "Making Noise." I began speaking through the tears:

"For many years, I heard the phrase 'body, mind, spirit' to describe what makes up 'me,' but I never got the message to value my body in the same way I honored my mind through study and my spirit through prayer. I chose to disconnect from my body after a pattern of sexual assault that began when I was young and continued into my forties. I was not friends with my vagina, and until I starting researching my orgasm at age forty-five; I was clueless about my body's potential to feel good.

"One of the most challenging things for me during my orgasm research was speaking up for myself. For years I had stayed quiet, whether it was about something that didn't feel good in bed or about someone who hurt me. I ignored the power and truth in my voice as much as I ignored the desires of my vagina. We were both lonely.

"I always stayed quiet when my boyfriends made love to me. I never asked for what I wanted. I willingly offered my body, even when what they were doing to me didn't feel good. I was a master at disconnecting from my body to protect myself from feeling any

sensations that could elicit the shame and pain from the original abuse.

"When I started my orgasm research and forced myself to be present with my feelings and the sensations in my body, I finally had to give a voice to my orgasm. She liked to speak up—not too loud, but she wanted to be respected, and I realized that by staying quiet all those years, I was dishonoring my body and my voice. I was not respecting my essence. I was not listening.

"In my research, I found by inhaling deep into my pelvis and humming or moaning on the exhale, I could feel more of my orgasmic sensations. Using my voice allowed my orgasm to go from being a short, quick release, like men experience, to waves of orgasmic climaxes. The full, deep, circular breaths send fresh oxygen into my genitals, and the sounds vibrate from my throat down my spine, through the walls of my vagina and out through my clitoris. Each cycle of breath and sound extends my orgasm longer and takes my body higher into an ecstatic state, expanding my orgasm from seconds to minutes to hours. It's my choice. I just have to use my voice.

"Tantra teacher Charles Muir said, 'In America, most women make more sound eating their dessert than they do in orgasm.' We definitely need to get more comfortable using our voices! Making sounds and giving verbal cues improve the quality and length of our orgasm. It's also a way of letting our partners know we approve of what they are doing. If you don't have a partner, allow your orgasm to speak

during self-pleasuring. By not making noise we are disowning our voices and our bodies and missing out on feeling all of our orgasm. The consequences of staying quiet can go way beyond having a satisfying orgasm.

"In my book Autobiography of an Orgasm, *I wrote candidly about my experience of being sexually assaulted many times and not speaking up because of the shame and judgment I knew I might face. It was something 'we just don't talk about,' and I thought I was the only one who had experienced it. I finally told my story because I wanted to give a voice to the six-year-old who was too confused and afraid to speak up. I also wanted to honor the forty-year-old woman in me who was raped during a party and still stayed quiet. I'm not too sure the man, who was intoxicated, thinks what he did was wrong because I never said anything. It was another secret that I kept to myself until a few years later, when another friend mentioned that she felt he had raped her. As sad as I was for her experience of assault by the same man, it was a relief that I wasn't alone. And then I wondered, what if I'd spoken up sooner? What if I'd said something to him so he knew his behavior was not acceptable? Maybe it would have saved my friend. Maybe it would have saved others.*

"One of the letters I received from a woman in her thirties who read Autobiography of an Orgasm *described her disconnection from her body after rape and assault in college: 'I can't even begin to express how much I was affected by your book. It brought up so much for me. I have never seen myself as worthy of enjoying life in general, and being*

sexually satisfied was definitely not even a blip on my radar. My mother was hateful and angry all the time from being raped in her youth, and so I grew up always hearing about how horrible men were. Then I went off to college where I was held in a frat boy's room against my will, where numerous guys molested me, followed by laughter and mocking. The icing on the cake was that they used razors to cut me so I would be ugly to everyone else. They said they would be the only people who would want to see me naked. I am covered in scars, and for a long time I believed them, and if I am being honest, I guess I still do. I don't talk about this story very much (pretty much never), so it is surprising me that I am telling it to you now.'

"It's estimated that 90% of acquaintance rapes don't speak up, and many of these happen in high school or the first years of college where alcohol is a factor in 90% of the cases. We are seeing more and more stories of girls committing suicide after being assaulted by someone they know or dying as a result of a night of extreme partying. In too many of these cases there are other people around taking photos or videos or helping dispose of the body, but rarely is someone speaking up and saying 'Stop' or 'Let me get you home safely and stay with you until you are better.'

"There was another incident of assault that I didn't write about in my book because he was a popular lama with many followers. I admired the message he brings to the western world, but I stopped admiring the messenger when this lama groped me and pushed his tongue into my mouth. Up until that moment, I had never touched

this man; I had only treated him with reverence, bowing when I saw him out of respect for his position. At the time, I was making a film about him. When the uninvited groping happened, I was meeting him in his room to take him to where I would be interviewing him a few minutes later. After I pushed him away, I didn't say a word except, 'We are ready for the interview.' And then I walked out and spent the next thirty minutes interviewing him on camera. I didn't mention the incident in his room a few minutes earlier.

"I was thirty-nine, and what I can say is that my body and mind went into 'shock' mode. I just focused on what I was supposed to do— interview this man for a documentary. Later I mentioned what had happened to my boyfriend at the time, and to my cameraman, and to another friend who was a photographer on the project. I even continued to work on the film a little longer until I heard from another woman that she felt this lama had also taken advantage of her. I finally stopped making the film, because every time I saw this man's face on screen, I felt violated. Part of me wondered if maybe I just didn't understand his culture; maybe he didn't mean to force himself on me. Later I found out it had happened to other women too.

"Recently, I watched a CNN story on Bikram Choudhury, the founder of the Bikram yoga movement. He was responding to allegations of rape by several of his former students. I know two of those students, and I believe that he raped them. His response to the charges was that he doesn't need to sexually assault anyone because so many women love him, he wouldn't have to force himself on any of

them. Through his tears he added, 'Shame on western culture' for doing this to him. That statement sent a surge of rage through my body.

"The poet Maya Angelou wrote, 'I come as one, I stand as 10,000.' We as women and the men who love us can't afford to not speak up anymore. There is power in our voices. We need to remember our bodies as sacred no matter what has happened to us. And we need to remember to choose love over fear when making decisions on whether to reveal ourselves. I am done being shamed and being quiet, and I know I am not standing alone. The only way to honor my body is to speak up and make noise, whether it's to stop the ongoing assault of girls and women or to bring my orgasm to climax."

After I finished, the room was quiet. I was supposed to offer a Q&A session, but the room felt lethargic with tension, like the energy had been zapped out of everyone. It was like when you go numb watching the news of a tragedy; we had no place to put our discomfort. Instead I thanked everyone for coming and let them know the writers would be signing the books. I walked to the back of the room to say goodbye to my mother and my kids. The kids hugged me, but Mom stepped away. I don't think it was conscious, but it felt like she was ashamed of me or ashamed of what had happened to me even though none of it was my fault or her fault. Why do we always search for people to blame?

Later Dan Wakefield wrote about the event: *"(The) women read from their stories included in the book* Autobiographies of Our

Orgasms. *All were powerful and went far beyond the physical to the mental, emotional and moral experiences of women . . . this may be an event that goes down in cultural history, like Alan Ginsburg's reading of 'Howl' at a gallery in San Francisco in the fifties. I missed that one but was glad to be at this one."*

I found it hard to sleep that night. There was another event scheduled in Los Angeles in a few weeks. I had been so moved watching *Vagina Monologues*, where you heard women speaking other women's stories, and the crowd cried, cringed, and cheered along with the storytellers. Now I was asking women to speak their own stories of vulnerability. Telling the truth about my sensual path out loud was making me feel naked and uncomfortable. I wanted to stay covered.

A few days later I left Indiana, packing two suitcases to last me through planned work and travels to Dallas, Los Angeles, New York, London, and Zimbabwe during the next six months. I'd also signed up to go on a Qoya retreat to Bali, a place I'd wanted to return to since my first trip in 2002. I didn't bother to organize any of the boxes that had been packed or even to pack the rest of my closet. I was honoring my agreement with Ben. It had been eight months since I had moved out of the house. I was not going to move the rest of my things until the house was sold and I received a payment so I could find another home. I made my bed and drove to the airport.

TWELVE

The French call orgasm *la petite mort*, the little death. I'd been practicing my bliss sessions for six months, so I guess I was dying a bit every day and at the same time, my body was feeling healthier than ever.

One of the biggest changes I noticed was in my breath. From my study of somatic bodywork, I knew that changing my breath was the quickest way to change my health. We are chronic under-breathers; we take shallow breaths that prevent our bodies from fully functioning. I noticed that my inhale was short and barely filled my lungs. My exhale was even shorter. With the bliss sessions, I was breathing deep into my pelvis, flooding the area with fresh oxygen. The deep exhales made my body relax and soften. My breathing after the sessions became more conscious, too, and I saw how years of shallow breathing had affected everything from my energy to my digestion.

My breath was activating more than my orgasm. I saw how my willingness to breathe deeper made me more present, both in the moment and in my body. It made sense that for the years I'd felt damaged from abuse, I'd ignored my breath, only allowing in a little oxygen at a time. Now, I was experiencing more of myself, and of life, just by taking deeper breaths. During each orgasm, each *petite mort*, my exhalation from the orgasm was followed by an inhalation into aliveness.

On July 3, 2015, I was in Dallas spending a few days with Dee, a best friend from college, before I went on to Los Angeles to join all four of my children for the wedding of my niece. Since I'd been living on the road for eight months, I'd left suitcases at friends' homes in Miami, Indianapolis, and Dallas. I would collect pieces of my life as I returned to each place.

It was the day before July 4th, not a day for much online communication, but I checked my emails and received a newsletter from Kaci Florez, one of the women who had been in my Qoya Teachers' Intensive earlier in the year in Costa Rica. Kaci was only twenty-nine, and she was a wise soul in a young body. Any time I partnered with her for an activity during the Intensive, she talked about her husband, Jhonny Florez, a world champion BASE-jumper. He literally jumped off mountains and flew like a bird in a wing-suit designed to let him fly using only his arms and legs to guide him. The other thing that impacted me was how much in love they were. I'd been divorced for sixteen years at that point and forgot what love could feel like. I was halfway through my year of bliss sessions and really enjoying getting to know the nuances of my body and my orgasm. Listening to Kaci's stories about Jhonny made me remember the sweetness of intimacy with another person. I had to wait six more months before I could experience that again.

Kaci was an intriguing writer. She occasionally sent out newsletters, and I always made a point of reading them. Her July 3rd newsletter invited us to explore liberation, explore our freedom:

"Imagine what it would be like to soar over the mountain tops like a bald eagle . . . what would you see? How would it feel? Oh, the inspiration . . .

"I hope that as we go into this holiday weekend of celebrating our country's independence, each of us can take a moment to honor the feeling of freedom that is at our essence. Honor the feeling of living as an independent being, free to make our own choices, have our own thoughts, love who we wish to love, and be who we are born to be. How much we choose to receive our gifts of freedom is entirely up to us. Our biggest obstacle to receiving these gifts often resides in our choice. And so again, regardless of what your relationship to freedom is, I encourage each of you to try the following ritual at some point over the next few days:

"Find a quiet space where you can take a few slow, deep breaths. Allow your breath to bring you into the present moment. Then use your imagination to think about and feel the essence of freedom. This can stem from an image or story from your past, or it can just be a pure feeling. Breathe into that feeling for a few moments. Do this at least until it feels good or pure. Then continue as long as it feels necessary. Perhaps add some free movement with your body. Simply move, sway, rock, dance however your body wants to. Continue doing this with

that sense of freedom. And do this for as long as feels good. When you feel like you are done, be sure to express gratitude for this experience. You can thank whatever or whomever you wish. You can thank your dance, yourself, your god, or whatever else is on your heart.

"The point is to pay attention to what IS there, not what is lacking."

I loved her invitation to: *"Honor the feeling of living as an independent being, free to make our own choices, have our own thoughts, love who we wish to love, and be who we are born to be. How much we choose to receive our gifts of freedom is entirely up to us."* I smiled as I closed the email, grateful for the unexpected gift of Kaci's words as I was finding the process of living without a home and with less stuff liberating.

A few hours later, Kaci wrote a message on a private FB page for our Qoya Intensive group. *Jhonny is gone,* she wrote. I read it several times because it didn't make sense.

Jhonny is gone. Jhonny is gone. Jhonny is gone.

I went back and re-read her email newsletter. She must have written it before she heard the news of her husband's death, but the opening line gave me the chills: *"Imagine what it would be like to soar over the mountain tops like a bald eagle . . ."*

Her husband died in a BASE-jumping accident on a mountain in Switzerland. As word got out, Facebook filled with hundreds of friends and family posting condolences from all over the world. They each had a special Jhonny story. I'd only met Jhonny through Kaci's stories about him and now I was meeting him through hundreds of posts honoring his life. He sounded like someone who embodied love and left behind a huge legacy. I was heartbroken for Kaci, now a young widow, as she flew to Switzerland to bring his body home.

The body.

We bury or cremate bodies. We talk about having a body, mind, and soul. Where do the mind and soul go after death? I'd been with three people when they died. My friend Sheri died of ovarian cancer in 2005. I slept in a bed next to her in hospice during the evenings; her husband Scott stayed with her during the days. She'd been in and out for weeks, holding on much longer than the doctors expected. The night before she died, she started speaking to someone in the room. I looked, but no one was there. It was the middle of the night. I asked her who it was. She said it was her father. I knew he was already dead. "He's right there," she said. I believed her.

I was with my godfather Bill when he died only a few months after discovering he had prostate cancer. He spent his life as a radiologist, helping to diagnose other people. How had he missed the signs? His cancer was advanced, and his decline was rapid. Within a few months, hospice was called to my godparents' home. My daughter Lucy was a newborn, and Sam was two years old, so they would come over for a while and sit next to his bed, just like

I had done when my godmother was sick with meningitis when I was young. I used to sing "You Are My Sunshine" to her.

My godsister Cathy lived an hour away, but my other godsister Wendy lived in Seattle. We called to let her know her father was rapidly declining, and she should come to say goodbye. Wendy had sent a bottle of water from Lourdes, France, known for being healing water, even bringing on miracles. The bottle sat next to Bill's bed.

Hospice delivered a hospital bed that we set up in the living room. His prized Steinway piano sat quietly in the other room, never to be played by him again.

Hospice sent nurses and Betty sent them home. They were not needed. Betty was a former nurse, and I watched her lovingly care for her husband of fifty years even as his body was shutting down. She rarely slept those days, always checking on Bill to see if he needed anything at all hours of the day and night. Towards the end, he couldn't tell us. One afternoon, as I was helping Betty change the sheets on the bed, a process that took two of us, Sam played with toys nearby while Lucy, only four months old, slept. Betty would roll Bill onto his side, and I would pull the sheets off and then tuck in new ones before Betty gently rolled Bill back onto the fresh sheets. If needed, we did this several times a day to make sure he was clean and dry. I'd just finished tucking Bill in when I noticed my son Sam was drinking from the bottle of holy water. He didn't know what it was, he was just thirsty. I grabbed the bottle; there were only a few drops left. I sprinkled them on Bill's head and body. He rested peacefully.

It was good to know he wasn't in pain. He'd taken care of me my whole life when I was sick; it was an honor to be with him at the end of his. When Bill first told me about his cancer, he mentioned he had the medicines at the house if the cancer became unbearable and he needed to end his life. He didn't need the medicine. I believe he willed himself to die quickly and spare himself and Betty an uncomfortable death.

My husband, Ben, was so supportive during this time. Ben organized hospital equipment and food for the house, and behind the scenes he took extra care of our two children so I could support my godparents.

A few days later, Bill's breathing slowed down even more. It was minutes between breaths. Finally, as he took an inhale, a deep gargling sound came from him on the exhale. I waited for the next inhale. Nothing. Betty and I weren't sure if he was gone, so she got Bill's stethoscope, the one with which I'd first listened to my own heartbeat—and Bill's—when I was little. This time when I put it to his chest, it was silent.

My Mom's husband John was the last person whose death I witnessed. Synchronicity allowed me to be with John on that day. He'd been declining, but his death was still unexpected. When I got the phone call that he'd been moved to the hospital, I was only a few hours' drive away. He was still in the ER when I arrived. My Mom looked scared and exhausted, but she didn't cry. The hospital didn't think he would make it much longer. We didn't want him to die there. The decision was made to move him to hospice, which was only a few miles away. Mom went home to rest as I drove in a van with John on a stretcher to hospice. The driver asked what music John like so we listened to classical music on the way.

I called Mom after he was settled in a room at the hospice center and asked her to come back over. The hospice staff had set up an extra bed in the room for her, but she climbed into bed with John and wrapped her body around his. He was lying on his side and I sat next to him holding his hand. As I watched Mom embracing John, I felt and saw an essence—a soft light—from John merge with my mother. When the soul leaves the body, maybe part of it merges into loved ones so that a piece of them always exists.

After I got Kaci's message about Jhonny passing, I knew she would find a way to honor her grief and remember that the first and last breath he ever took in life still existed. Keep breathing, I wanted to tell her. I had to remember to do the same.

THIRTEEN

I spent July sleeping in six different beds as I moved between cities. My body was exhausted from the constant switching of homes, and I was not doing the bliss sessions as much. There was so much sadness to hold that it seemed unimportant to nurture my sensual energy. At the end of the month, I went back to Indiana for a few weeks to help my son Willie with a move to Chicago. He was doing stand-up, and there was no better place for a young comic to be than the Chicago comedy scene. Ever since Willie was young, he made people laugh. He was a master storyteller and always kept the room engaged. I hoped the move would help him leave behind some of the sadness of his time at college in Boulder, Colorado and losing his roommate and dear friend Ryan during the beginning of his sophomore year. Like me when I was younger and hiding my sadness, I supposed that Willie could be doing the same, acting like everything was okay. I planned to keep checking in on him and making visits to Chicago every few months.

In September, I left for the Qoya retreat in Bali. I flew to the Sacramento airport first to meet Kaci Florez, who was going to join us in Bali for the retreat. Kaci was courageous enough to take her grief out into the world. She frequently shared revealing posts on social networking about her grief and being a young widow. Her entries were so intimate that you almost wanted to look away, but her words connected with anyone who had experienced loss. It seemed that as she spoke her truth, we were all healing unexpressed grief from our own losses in our lives.

After the retreat led by Rochelle Schieck, we spent a few extra days together in Bali first going to a full moon Agni Hotra, a fire ceremony that was supposed to be healing to the participants and to the Balinese living in the area. I was feeling less settled, so during the ceremony I silently asked for healing for my body and for my living situation. It had been eleven months since I left my home with the exception of my brief stays as it sat nearly empty. I'd slept in more than thirty different beds during that time and several nights on airplanes as I travelled to my next destinations, never going home. My body was craving to be in one place for a while, but I needed the money from the sale of my home to make it happen. Ben continued to give me some money each month to live on but not enough to get a home. My house had still not been put on the market.

One of the places we stayed after the retreat was a magical property called Bambu Indah, an eco-resort designed with the land and preservation in mind. The homes were made out of bamboo or wood; they were surrounded by lush gardens that produced the food we ate. I started to feel good again there. Our last night at Bambu Indah, I said a silent wish that I'd return by the end of the year. The end of the year would also mark the end of my year of the bliss sessions.

I flew back to the US and committed to finding a place to call home. I knew it would have to be after my annual trip to Zimbabwe that was six weeks away.

FOURTEEN

In November, I flew to Zimbabwe for the twenty-third time since 2008. I was hosting a Qoya Service and Safari Retreat. We would be living at a wildlife conservation park during the retreat and contributing to the local community. The donations from the retreat would go towards projects to help improve the lives of children, including paying school fees for under-privileged kids, providing new uniforms and schools supplies, and buying bicycles so they could have transport to school. We were contributing towards building a solar-powered library and community center, and would also be donating to the anti-poaching programs in the area, protecting the endangered rhinos and elephants.

I'd first flown to Zimbabwe in 2008. I'd never been anywhere in Africa, but when an acquaintance asked if I was interested in adopting a baby from there, it seemed like a miracle. I'd always wanted more children. I never expected my last son, Charlie, to be the last baby I'd hold or nurse. When I brought up the possibility of adopting Loveness from Zimbabwe, I showed her photo to my children, all teenagers, and then to Ben, who offered to help me raise Loveness as one of our own. We were ten years post-divorce, but we still supported each other.

"I'm not interested in having any more children," he told me at the time. "But I'll support you through this. I want the baby to feel like she is one of our children."

Loveness had been abandoned in a hot, dry field where a farmer noticed her, picked her up, and put her tiny body in his dirty wheelbarrow. She was less than two weeks old. The man pushed her through the field and onto the pothole-riddled street that led to the hospital. When he got to the hospital, he pushed the wheelbarrow all the way into the area accepting patients. For Zimbabwe, this was not a shocking sight. An acquaintance happened to be at the hospital when Loveness arrived and called me because she knew I was interested in adopting a baby. Her call seemed like a miracle. I got on a plane three weeks later.

The journey was twenty-two hours. When I changed planes in Johannesburg for the final flight, I sent Ben a text: *In less than four hours, I'll be holding Loveness. Thank you for supporting me.* Ben and my family sent me to Zimbabwe with good wishes and also concerns as it was the height of an economic collapse in Zimbabwe and a huge cholera outbreak. The week before I departed, a United Nations team concerned about human rights issues, including former President Jimmy Carter, were not granted visas for a visit.

Four days before I was supposed to leave, I opened *The New York Times* and saw a lengthy story that Zimbabwean President Robert Mugabe had denied visas to others:

"Mr. Mugabe's decision to forbid a humanitarian visit by Mr. Carter, former United Nations Secretary General Kofi Annan and Graça Machel, Nelson Mandela's wife, was a measure of the Zimbabwean leader's disdain for international opinion at a time when deepening hunger, raging hyperinflation and the collapse of health, sanitation and education services have crippled Zimbabwe."

The message was clear: Westerners were not welcome there. My stepfather, John Williams, advised me to consider adopting from a more stable country. I appreciated his concern, but the opportunity to adopt ten years after losing a baby seemed like a miracle—and I was ready for one.

I landed in Zimbabwe excited to meet the baby, but when I saw the woman waiting at the airport to collect me, I felt something was wrong. My stomach clenched, and my throat tightened.

Out of the blue, I said to her, "She's dead."

She nodded her head yes.

I avoided seeing Loveness's body for the entire eight days of the trip. While I was in shock from arriving to the news of her death, everyone else in Zimbabwe, including the doctor and his wife whom I was staying with, treated the news with an almost indifferent attitude. After a few days, especially in the middle of a cholera crisis, I finally understood why. There were tragic deaths happening daily. "Just choose another baby," the doctor said to me. "But don't think you can save every child here."

The day before I was to leave the country, I got permission to bury Loveness. "Do you want to see her?" a nurse asked me. I nodded. I'd come all this way to hold her; I promised myself I would do it before I left.

At this point, her body had been in the morgue for almost two weeks. It was summer in Zimbabwe with temperatures in the 80s. There was no air conditioning in the house where I was staying. There was definitely no air conditioning in the morgue.

To get there, I passed through the hospital waiting room, where mothers and grandmothers held sick children in their arms and usually another child asleep on their backs, secured to their bodies with a large cloth. I was the only white person at the hospital. Some children stared. It may have been the first time they'd ever seen a white person.

The morgue that was supposed to hold thirty bodies was overflowing with ninety bodies. "There is no place to put them, and people have no money to bury their loved ones," said the male nurse at the entrance of the morgue. He sat at a desk, his skin and uniform damp from the intense heat. I could see from his office through to the next room where the feet of the dead bodies were lined up. He waved me into another room where a white casket I'd picked out was placed in the middle of the room. I'd been asked the day before if it was okay to bury four other unclaimed dead babies with her. "Of course," I said.

The nurse opened the casket, and I stared at the bodies of five dead babies, each one wrapped in a white cloth. I'd only seen two photos and one video of Loveness alive, but I instantly knew which one she was in death. Loveness was in the middle of the casket with the bodies of four dead boys around her. One of the biggest regrets of my life was being too afraid to touch her when I saw her. I looked at her and the other dead babies for a minute as I held my hand over my mouth and nose. I could still smell and taste the decaying bodies in the morgue. The mother in me wanted to hold her, to do what I had come all this way to do, but instead I turned around and went outside so I could take a breath of fresh air.

It took me a few days before I could send a text to Ben and tell him the news. It was like I wanted to keep the dream alive, because who would I be after this dream died?

Before I left the country, a friend in Zimbabwe warned me about speaking or writing publically about the conditions in Zimbabwe. "If you want to return," he said, "Don't speak out against the government." I knew that journalists and activists had been jailed, tortured and even killed for writing about the human rights violations in the country. I wanted to return again to help the children and the endangered animals so I chose to remain quiet. As someone who was finally speaking up about what mattered in my life, this time I knew my silence would be an effective way for me to continue to return and help in small ways for the marginalized voices in Zimbabwe.

FIFTEEN

When I arrived back in the US after the Qoya Zimbabwe Retreat in November of 2015, I was sure Ben and I could come to some sort of resolution. I'd been living without a home for over a year. It was the home we'd gather to celebrate birthdays and holidays and summer vacations together. Now, my children were watching me live without a home. My children had no place to gather as a family, at least with their mother.

I also wasn't invited on the annual Christmas family ski trip that I'd first started planning fifteen years earlier. Ben and I had taken the trip together every year post-divorce as a way to share the holiday with our children. But after Ben began a relationship with Annie, I was uninvited on the trip.

In 2015, I decided to spend Christmas with my mother in Naples, Florida. We'd had a tough year since the book came out. For a few months I didn't speak to her after not feeling supported. My mother also expressed her concern over my living situation. She continually reminded me that I couldn't blame anyone except myself.

I missed her husband, John, who died the year before. My dad died in 1988, when I was twenty-five. John had come into Mom's life when she was in her early seventies and I was in my early forties. When they married, I called him my soul father because he was so much more than a stepfather. John always spoke to me with empathy and compassion. He also understood that children, even grown ones, sometimes just needed to be heard. He listened deeply.

John could see that Ben had been trying to push me out of my home and maybe even my family, and he also could see a bigger picture for me beyond that home. Here is one of the last emails he ever wrote to me:

"Betsy, dear, you are on our minds. I don't have any insights into what you are going through, but surely [there] is a lot of hurt going around.

Let me pass on a little experience . . . that I have found uplifting.

As required by my heart doctor in Evanston, I am in the early stages of a 12-week program for patients who have had cardiac surgery. In order for this to happen, I have had the services of an intelligent woman about 51 years old who migrated west from Sri Lanka a good many years ago. She drives me to my rehab sessions and brings me home.

She has brought to mind the striking Indian woman Arundati Roy, a native of the Kerala area of India who became quite well known by an early novel, The God of Small Things. *After its success she became active politically. I shan't write more about her, but encourage you to look at her web site and to look at her Wikipedia images. The article itself has a picture of her lecturing at Harvard last year.*

I hope that the text and the images may be supportive of you in your work for a better world.

Love,

John"

I read Arundhati Roy's book, *The God of Small Things*, wondering if John was giving me pieces of a story of my own life that I needed to witness. Would it be possible to not let a series of small decisions affect my bigger life purpose? In the book, Arundhati Roy writes about great stories having no secrets. It made me look at the areas of my life where I was still being silenced.

My body had healed from the past damage. I'd released two books in the past year while living without a home. I noticed that I was super healthy after the year. Even with all the international travel, I never got sick. Except for the heartache around my family, I was content.

I started doing the bliss sessions again and noticed how my body responded enthusiastically, like they had never stopped. I was feeling more sensual than ever, like the wings of a hummingbird were constantly fluttering in my pussy. However, there was a piece of my family that felt undone, and I wasn't sure how to put it back together. That Christmas, I wished for resolution with my family, but Ben ignored my requests to share the holiday.

I decided to return to the one place that made my body feel most alive. I booked a ticket for Bali. I would be there for the New Year.

SIXTEEN

I woke up in Bali on the first day of 2016 ready to continue my bliss sessions. Even though there had been a party where I stayed the night before, I went to bed early, still jet-lagged from the twenty-four hours of travel. My first morning waking up in Bali, my hands automatically began to give my body a self-massage, which was like foreplay for the bliss sessions. These near daily massages were like taking a vitamin. My body was healthier with them. At some point during the past year, my practice expanded to include finding pleasure in my hands, so during the self-massage, I was engaging both my hands *and* the body part I was touching in receiving intoxicating sensations.

It had been thirteen months since I'd had sex with a man. I was feeling so good in my body that I decided to extend my bliss sessions another six months, maybe even a year. I'd heard that you kept the imprint of partners you have sex with in your body for several months. Now my body was a sanctuary—and I loved the autonomy.

In the past, if I'd been without sex for several months, my longings shut down, and I didn't even crave it. With my commitment to listening to the wisdom and desires of my body over the past year, even on the days or weeks that I didn't take time for the bliss sessions, I still found that I stayed in a state of turn-on. There was a subtle throbbing in my genitals that heightened if I focused on the sensation. Just by taking a deeper breath, the throbbing would expand. I'd also read that as women age, the body stops focusing on reproduction and starts focusing on self-cultivation and nourishing the internal organs and nervous system that support orgasm. I was definitely finding that to be true. During clitoral orgasms, I used to have to focus mostly on the clit and a tiny area just around it. Now I could expand my orgasm by rubbing the areas of the clitoris that connect down from the tip on the inside, like a wishbone. Where formerly there was only numbness, or stroking my clit felt like glass shards, now my entire pussy would vibrate within minutes of attention, longing for more exploration. I'd take my time, slowly enjoying the touch of my fingers first outside and then inside my vagina. As the orgasm grew, my chest would arch as if my heart was expanding. My inhale deepened as my hips softened and opened. I knew some people needed to fantasize during self-pleasure, but my concentration was only on feeling my touch and then seeing if I could do anything to make it feel even better. Never once did I think of a man during these sessions.

Returning to Bali was like returning to remembering my essence that I had found and then lost somewhere between sleeping in so many different beds in 2015. The death of my friend Kaci's husband also left me aware of my own unexpressed grief from so many deaths early in my life. Kaci was modeling to me how to dance with the grief and honor the sadness. In Bali, I remember her wails one night. The sun had just set, and suddenly a primal roar came from her room. *Let it out,* I prayed for her. *It's safe to cry here. Don't keep it inside and let yourself slowly die with him.*

Now I was back in Bali just two months after dreaming of returning. I was waking up in an antique home outside of Ubud, Bali on the property of Bambu Indah. The home I was sleeping in was over a hundred years old and had been a gift from a nobleman to his bride. The house was just one room that was big enough for a full-size canopy bed and a dresser. I stepped out a back door into a private, open-air bathroom. I turned on the shower and stepped in. Walls of bamboo protected the area, but the top was open. I looked up at the blue morning sky as water ran over my body.

In a month, I would be fifty-three. Even after the birth of my four children, I'd always had a flat stomach but now there was an added roundness to my hips and belly. I'd quit my intense Ashtanga yoga and running practices two years ago after my body was telling me to let it soften. I'd run into my former yoga instructor in Miami a few months ago, and he asked me if I was pregnant. I joked that I was in my fifties and my body was changing so he wouldn't feel uncomfortable after asking, but it did make me think about all the times in the recent years that people—mostly men—chose to comment on my weight.

"You're putting on some pounds," one of the men I respected told me. "You need to lose some weight."

During a course at a spiritual retreat center, a man I'd just met told me, "You need to lose twenty pounds. You're holding onto extra weight as protection." Other than discussing the films we'd been watching together that week, I'd never invited him into a more intimate conversation with me, but still he felt okay commenting on how I looked.

"You'd look better if you lost some weight," another man suggested.

All of these comments came to me unsolicited.

Women made comments too. A woman putting make-up on me for an event said, "You're slightly overweight." And I wondered what is this number or way of thinking that defines us as just right or too thin or too big or slightly overweight? Some of my friends had experienced radical weight loss by taking Adderall, the same pill they were having prescribed for their children so they would pay attention in school. It's a Schedule II narcotic, like cocaine.

When I was thinner, it came through an unhealthy combination of Prozac washed down with a glass of wine every night, but everyone told me how great I looked even though on the inside I was empty.

I was now in my early fifties, healthy and feeling at peace in my body, and I was being told that I wasn't good enough based on these men's ideal weight for me. I lived in a world that didn't want women to feel good in their bodies. My commitment to honor and enjoy my body at this point felt like a rebellious act. I dismissed their comments and bought a bigger pair of jeans. I refused to define myself by numbers or size, but it still bugged me that I existed in a culture that valued me more when I weighed less.

Bali is called "The Land of Gods." It seemed like the perfect place to discover the spiritual knowledge beneath my skin and the mysteries of the universe within my body. I didn't venture out much while I was there. I was so happy to have a home for a month. I stayed mostly on the Bambu Indah property, going on trash walks in the morning to clean up the river and village surrounding the property. It felt right to be giving back and caring for the land I was living on.

I was also editing a second anthology of readers' stories, *Autobiographies of Our Orgasms 2,* which was to be released in the spring. I decided to feature only women's voices in this anthology. Although the *O* books weren't focused solely on women who had experienced sexual assault, at least half of the stories I received were from women writing about being molested, many when they were younger. Some of the women were sharing their stories for the first time, and I knew how vulnerable they felt to finally speak up. I also knew there was the chance family and friends wouldn't believe them, or they'd be questioned, "Why did you wait so long?" instead of being told, "Thank you for speaking up."

Six months earlier, thirty-five of Bill Cosby's accusers were on the cover of *New York* magazine. One of the women had kept the secret of her alleged assault for over forty years. I would be curious to know any health conditions the women experienced. I know the body holds onto our history unless we make an effort to heal.

One of the most powerful stories in the second anthology was by poet Rebecca Holt who wrote for the first time about being molested by someone close to her family:

"I have realized over time that I would go unconscious during my abuse. These experiences happened over several years during the ages of 3-6. I had symptoms throughout my life of fainting and always wondering if something had happened to me. I would repeatedly ask my mom all of the time if she could remember anything. Deep down I always knew, my body knew. The memories were deeply locked away, and would come out in my dreams at times at night. After some of my more vibrant memories began to emerge, working with a therapist and body worker around the age of twenty-five, I went over one night to a relative's house to visit and sleep over. Randomly, the man who had abused me was visiting my relative's house. I went to bed that night and upon waking the next morning, it was as if I had been riding a horse for two years as hard as I could. My entire groin area was exhausted, and I could feel it crying from its core. My body was

obviously letting me know . . . it was tightening to protect me and was reeling from the shock that was lingering throughout my body."

Rebecca's story in the book mixes song lyrics and poems with essay to create an anthem for women to speak up. Chills went through my body when I read her words:

When we rise from our own power and use our soul voice

to stand up and to be counted, in the truest, most beautiful

expression of who we are.

The world joins us in our symphony!

I had found my voice and was committed to creating a safe and nurturing space for women to use their voices too. The anthologies were becoming a place where we could rise together rooted in connection.

SEVENTEEN

I left Bali after a month to return to my beloved Byron Bay, Australia. I would be there for my 53rd birthday and for the annual One Billion Rising event. Instead of doing *Vagina Monologues*, the local V Day organizers chose to put on *Vagina Conversations*, an evening of stories featuring local storytellers. I was one of the selected speakers. The local newspaper ran an article about the event titled "Talking Twats!" It was a bigger production than the spoken word events I hosted for my book in the US. The evening was sold out. Three hundred people gathered to listen to ten women speak the truth of their sensual paths. After the event, almost everyone stayed for a Q&A. There was collective support for the truth in the room; no one wanted it to end.

When I was in Byron Bay the year before, the movie *Fifty Shades of Grey* was released. I resisted watching it because after my book release, others and myself were craving a more authentic conversation around sex.

I had no problem with the sex presented in the movie, if that's what turned you on. I would offer to women and men who have experienced unhealed abuse around their bodies in the past to slow down and see what sex feels like when the focus in only on feeling pleasure, not pain. Before I healed my body from the trauma of assault, I tended to have sex with men who liked it fast and hard. My body was numb anyway. After my choice to truly listen to my vagina—after so many years of ignoring her—I found she wanted sex that was slow and soft. The slower a man touched me, the more I could feel. When I shared this with a man prior to my year of abstaining from sex with a partner, there was a palpable relief in his energy, maybe because he knew he didn't have to perform for me; he just needed to be present and communicate. I will add that this man had one of the smallest penises I've ever been with, but it was truly one of the most sensual experiences of my life.

In Bali, I was still content being my own sensual muse. I was not longing for a man's touch because I was so satisfied with my own. I wondered when this spell would be broken.

By the end of February, it was time to head back to the US. I was teaching Qoya in Naples, Florida in March, Costa Rica in April, and Indianapolis in May.

When I arrived back in the States, I stayed with my mom at her Florida condo as I offered Qoya classes at a nearby studio. The women in class were mostly in their fifties to eighties. I love that Qoya has no levels, so anyone was welcome to come and participate. The idea was using movement to remember our essence, and often when I'd tell women there was no way they could do it wrong, they began to cry. They'd recognized they'd been "trying to do it right" their whole lives, which didn't always feel good in their bodies.

Qoya had been a key in unlocking my body as I healed from a lifetime of disconnection. Now I was fortunate to be offering classes, workshops, and retreats to women around the world. My mom had just turned 83 and came to two of my classes, but mostly she stayed home knitting and watching the news, which was becoming divisive in the midst of the upcoming presidential election. It was stunning to me that Donald Trump was building a platform of supporters. I'd never met him but witnessed interviews where he demonstrated disrespect towards women. I was shocked that he was popular. At the same time, it was encouraging to watch Lady Gaga perform her song "Til It Happens to You" during the Oscars. During the song, which is about sexual abuse, she was joined by dozens of women who were living beyond the wounds of past sexual assault. Women were starting to speak up and rise.

In Qoya and in my travels, I was having deep, connected conversations, even with my Uber or Lyft drivers. With Mom, I felt a lot of disapproval around how I was living. There was not much conversation, and she seemed unhappy and had low energy. During the week with her, I'd come in from a beach walk at 4:00 p.m., and she'd been eating dinner already, alone. Her husband John had been dead for three years, and I missed his presence in her life, in our lives. When John was alive, we'd have dinner together. One of my favorite things was listening to the two of them singing Broadway tunes at bedtime as I lay in the room next to them. Through the walls, I could hear them in bed singing to each other. I'd fall asleep to their harmonized voices. Now, the condo was either quiet or a steady dose of disturbing world news was on the TV.

The night before my final Qoya class in Naples, I got a text from Ali, a friend in Zimbabwe. At the time, I was on a video conference call with several Qoya teachers. In a few weeks, we would be co-leading a Qoya Collective Retreat in Costa Rica with each of us teaching a class during the week. Kaci, Lindsay, Sarah, Dana, Angharad, Fabiola, and Virginia were on the call too. Lindsey had missed the previous call because she was on a family vacation in the Bahamas with her husband, Tom, and their two boys, Patrick, age nine, and Logan, age five. We all got to share the trip virtually through the photos Lindsay posted on Facebook of them swimming with dolphins and playing in the sand. We had all been in the Qoya Intensive Training together the year before and had gotten even closer after Kaci's husband died. I was looking forward to gathering with them again. Fifty women from all over the world would be joining us. It would be the largest Qoya retreat so far.

In the middle of the call, my phone buzzed with the text from Ali.

GoGo died, he wrote.

Like reading the news of Kaci's husband death, the text didn't make sense to me. Gogo was a healer in Zimbabwe whom people came from as far as England to see. I knew GoGo had been sick, but she was younger than me. She couldn't be gone. I'd met her through Ali in 2011. In just six months, she was supposed to be a guest speaker at my annual Qoya Retreat in Zimbabwe. Sometimes GoGo and I visited each other in our dreams. She'd appear in my dreams and give me guidance. The night before I heard the news of her death, she came to me in a dream, just smiling and saying, "Everything is okay." My godmother Betty had said the same thing to me in a dream a few years after she died. "Everything is okay," she said. I woke up feeling like she'd been sitting next to me in bed.

Hearing the news of GoGo's death put me into a state of disbelief. It was evening, but I decided to go for a walk on the beach. I wanted to go put my feet in the water. One of the spirits GoGo channeled was a mermaid spirit who spoke multiple languages. Each time I returned to Zimbabwe, I'd bring GoGo (and the mermaid spirit) shells or a shell necklace from some beach in the world I had visited. She'd smile and place it at the altar of the room she used for readings and healings.

I walked out to the living room where Mom was knitting and watching the news.

"I'm going for a walk," I said. "I just heard that one of my friends died."

I don't know if she didn't hear me, maybe the TV was too loud, but she didn't look up. Mom was not good with death or illness. I believe her lack of connection during those times was due to her own unhealed grief of losing her first husband when she was twenty-four. At the time, Mom had a four-month-old, my oldest sister, Susan. They were living in San Diego when she got the news from the Navy that her husband died in a plane crash during training. Mom's parents flew out from Indiana, packed her up, and brought them home. Even sixty years later, I don't think she can *hear* bad news.

I walked the beach that night with the stars lighting the sand. I usually walked in the mornings as the sun warmed the beach. That night, the sand was cool on my bare feet. I picked up a shell and walked into the water up to my knees. I took several minutes to think of gratitude for GoGo, and then I brought the shell to my lips and blew those moments into the shell. When I was done, I threw the shell as far as I could into the still ocean. When it dropped into the water the shell made ripples that took several seconds to alter the water I was standing in. And then there she was—a dolphin's fin came out of the water about thirty feet in front of me and then disappeared. I waited a long time to see if it would surface again, but in my heart, I knew it was gone.

The next morning, Mom asked me to move items I had been storing at her condo. Since I'd been living without a home, I left some clothes at my mom's during a previous stay. She had two homes, one in Indiana, and one in Naples. Every closet was filled with her clothes and possessions. I was happy to be free of so much stuff, but I wasn't ready to part with two boxes of my things so I left them at Mom's. She said that she needed the space. I was stunned. I had shown up for Mom when she needed me, especially when John was dying, and now that I needed support, it felt like no one in my family was showing up for me. I'd stayed quiet all those years, not speaking up to my parents about the pain I was in after sexual assault. Even after my book was released, my family mostly ignored it.

The rage and tears filled me as I quickly packed my belongings. It was clear; I didn't feel welcome in my mother's home. My heart started racing and my breath got shallow. I didn't feel safe there, but I had no home to go to.

As Mom sat knitting and not saying a word, I put everything in my rental car, including the two boxes. Within ten minutes, I was ready to leave. I walked out her door without saying a word. She stayed quiet too. Before I drove off, I sat in my car in the parking lot of her condo building. The AC was on full blast, but I was sweating. I could hear her neighbors enjoying the pool. It was a beautiful day. I silently said to myself, *This feels like the end of my relationship with my mother. I may never see her again. Am I okay with that?* I listened for the answer, put the car in gear, and drove away.

I didn't know what to do or where to go. I called my college friend Dee, and she said, "Come to Dallas." I checked flights, and there was a flight out of Fort Lauderdale in three hours. It was a two-hour drive to the airport. With the extra boxes, I had too much luggage. I drove to the post office and sent the boxes to Dallas. It seemed like a miracle there was no line. A man opened the door for me each time I carried in a box. I couldn't do it on my own. My heartbeat was starting to go back to normal when a text came through from my Mom. It didn't say, *Come back and let's talk.* It didn't say, *I love you.* The text said, *You left two shoes.*

Part of me wanted to leave them. Instead, I wrote back, *Put them outside your door.* I drove back to my mom's, and the shoes weren't there. I walked in the door. "Your shoes are in the bedroom," I heard. I took seven steps to get to the bedroom, grabbed my shoes, and then seven steps to reach the door. I started to leave, and then a wave of fortitude surged through my bones. I was not comfortable living in this legacy of the feminine in my family where we stayed quiet. Holding a shoe in each hand, I walked over to where she was sitting.

I noticed Mom was trying to untangle a ball of yarn. She pulled at the loops of yarn, trying to find the place where it would unravel.

"Thank you for not standing for the women in our family, because it made me stand for myself," I said. As I walked away, she was silent.

I took a hard gulp when I left the condo like an old pattern was being cleared from my throat. The sun warmed my skin as I walked to my car. I looked at two different shoes I was holding. I hadn't left a pair. I'd left one shoe each of two pairs. One was leopard print, one was sparkly silver. I had no idea where the mates to the shoes were. I opened the trunk and tossed the shoes into one of my two suitcases that I'd been carrying for the past sixteen months.

My throat was dry as I drove out of the condo parking lot. If none of this had happened, I'd be on a beach walk by now. The night before, I'd seen a dolphin after my prayers for GoGo. I looked at the time; I had three hours before my flight. It would take two hours to get to the airport and a few minutes to drop my car and get my bags checked in. I thought I could make it as long as there was no traffic.

I chose to make a quick stop to get an iced tea for the road. As I walked in the restaurant, a man held the door for me, and as I passed he said, "Sorry." I looked at him and said thank you, not sure why he'd said, "Sorry."

I ordered my tea, and a few minutes later the girl who handed it to me said, "I'm sorry." She might have meant that it took so long? And then as I walked out the door, one more person said it to me, "I'm sorry."

What was going on? Why were people saying they were sorry? As I drove towards the airport, I silently said *thank you* after getting a feeling I knew whom the words were coming from.

I arrived in Dallas to a good meal prepared by my friend Dee and the offer of a closet and bedroom to use at her home. It always felt good to unpack my bags, even if only for a few days. I slept well the first two nights at the house. The events with my mom hurt. At the same time, I also felt empowered by being who I needed to be in that moment and not who she wanted me to be. It was clear I was not living the life she had dreamed for me.

I checked in with Ali to see what the plans were to bury GoGo. Ali had been a good friend since I met him on a plane to Zimbabwe in 2009. He'd been studying with GoGo for the past several years. They spent weeks together as he supported her during rituals and healings for people. I think in the end, she was transmitting to him everything she knew so that he could pass it on. Every time I went to Zimbabwe during the past five years, I made time to see her. I took her bags of clothes to pass out to all the children and women she supported in the nearby villages. If there was a Mother Teresa of Zimbabwe, it was GoGo. Her name meant grandmother, and she was everyone's spiritual grandmother.

I still couldn't believe she was gone. I remembered the dream I'd had just a few nights earlier—*everything is going to be okay*. A few hours later, I received an email from my friend Fabiola, who was co-leading the Qoya Collective Retreat in Costa Rica that was starting in two weeks. I read it once and closed my laptop, not able to handle the news. Kaci text me a few minutes later. "Did you read the email about Lindsay?" she wrote. My head dropped into my hands. I didn't want to acknowledge it, but it was true. Lindsay and her husband Tom were in the hospital with lung damage from smoke inhalation. Their home had burned to the ground during the night. As they woke up to the house on fire, Lindsay ran upstairs *into the fire* and got two young girls who were spending the night out of the house. Even as the house was dark and filled with smoke and flames, Lindsay put the two girls on her lap, slid down the stairs, and carried them outside into the safety of the night. No one was able to get to her boys in time. Patrick and Logan died in the fire.

EIGHTEEN

It did not feel like everything was going to be okay.

I did not care about having a home anymore. I'd been asked to leave my home eighteen months earlier, but suddenly it didn't seem to matter. In that time, I'd witnessed Kaci dancing in deep grief after losing her husband, then GoGo died, and now Lindsay's children were gone. In the news, I was seeing mothers trying to escape from the deadly war in Syria with their children. There was so much suffering in the world. How does one coexist with it but not get lost in the pain? How does one trust that even in the midst of the pain, love is present and will guide you home?

I hadn't spoken to my mother since I left her in Naples. It had been over six weeks when I received an email informing me and other family members that Mom hadn't been feeling like herself, and recent tests revealed that she had multiple myeloma, which affects the blood and bones. I knew from my study of BodyTalk energy medicine that this type of illness in the body could relate to not having a strong family structure, to not feeling like you belong. I called to check in on her and then prayed as I always did for radical healing within my own family.

It didn't seem possible that things could get any worse than that moment, but they did.

NINETEEN

There are some songs that I'm happy if I never hear again: "Kung Fu Fighting" and "Ebony and Ivory" come to mind. I'll always switch the channel on the radio before they get through the first verse.

I also dislike most everything by the Bee Gees. I like their personal style, and I like their harmonies, but I could never figure out how to dance to their music. I couldn't find the right beat. Maybe it's because I was coming of age in the seventies, and learning to groove to "Stayin' Alive" and "Jive Talkin'" was unnatural to my boyish teenage hips.

There was one song that made my hips happy and my heart soften: "Hey Jude" by The Beatles. I couldn't dance to it—I don't think anyone does—but it was a song that made me stop whatever I was thinking or doing or saying and reach over and turn up the volume on the radio.

The week I was graduating from high school, one of my close friends died in a tragic accident. As Laura lay sun tanning in her driveway, her mother pulled in, didn't see her, and ran over

Laura's body. We gathered a week later for Laura's funeral. Her class graduated the next week without her. None of the adults had any words to help us make sense of her death.

I spent that summer working as a lifeguard at a summer camp in southern Indiana. No one asked me how I was doing, and I wouldn't have known what to say if they'd asked. I listened to "Hey Jude" often, almost like I was willing Paul's voice to make it better. I wanted to believe him that it would be.

That summer I tried two things to make it better—sex and alcohol. I was considered a good girl, and Laura's death left me confused. I rebelled against the best parts of myself. The sex didn't work out. I kept my eyes shut tight as the man I'd chosen unzipped his pants. My hips froze. There was no music in the background, only the sounds of his grunts as he unsuccessfully poked around my clenched genitals. It was a relief when he gave up. I tried alcohol next. It was an airplane-sized bottle of vodka that I stole from my older sister's room. I mixed it with a 7-Up and slowly drank it, alone in my room, hoping it would erase my sadness.

The following semester I went away to college. The music of the '80s became more danceable with pop songs by Michael Jackson and Madonna. Their music played during my first wedding reception in 1985. By the time I divorced in 1987, I was listening to the new U2 album. The song "I Still Haven't Found What I'm Looking For" summed up how I was living. That is, until I met Ben.

The first marriage was brief; I don't remember if we had a favorite song. The second marriage was to Ben. Our first date, we talked for eight hours. Our second date, he took me to the local music store and we shopped for music. He bought me eight CDs: Joni Mitchell, The Police, Steve Winwood, Little Feat, Mac McNally, Tracy Chapman, U2, and Linda Ronstadt. He didn't like U2, but I added it to the pile anyway. As we were falling in love, we listened to Joni Mitchell's *Blue* album on repeat. One of the songs on it was probably playing when we got pregnant with our first child. By the time three more children were born in the next five years, we'd stopped listening to music together.

I don't remember listening to "Hey Jude" with Ben, but I do remember listening to it with our children. It was 1995, and our youngest, Charlie, was three months old. Willie was two, Lucy was four, and Sam was five. It was a cold and rainy Halloween night. Due to the weather, I took them trick-or-treating at a mall. The three older kids skipped from store to store, asking for candy as I pushed Charlie, who was dressed as a pumpkin, in the stroller. Ben wasn't with us. He'd come home late the night before. I found his jacket wadded up in the garage covered in vomit. I didn't mention it, and neither did he.

After wandering the mall for thirty minutes, the kids' buckets were heavy with candy. I decided to head home. Charlie would need to nurse again soon, and everyone would need dinner.

I pushed Charlie's stroller out to the car with the three kids holding hands. It was getting dark earlier, and safely navigating the parking lot with four children was challenging, especially in the cold, drizzling rain. I popped open the back of my red Volvo station wagon and unlocked the passenger door for kids to get in. Lucy, dressed like a dancing bear, quickly climbed across to the middle seat; she always tried to anticipate what I needed. She reached for Willie's candy-filled pumpkin container so that I could get him into his car seat. Willie was dressed like a wizard. Sam, dressed as a Power Ranger, stayed by my side as I lifted Charlie into his car seat. It began to rain harder, but Sam held onto the stroller until I got Charlie buckled into his seat. I shut the door and opened the front door for Sam. Usually he sat in the very back seat of the car, but that night I let him get in front.

My hair and clothes were already damp from the rain, so I quickly closed up the stroller and loaded it into the third seat of the Volvo. Charlie began to cry the minute I closed the tailgate. I knew he was hungry. *We'll be home in fifteen minutes*, I thought. The car ride will calm him down.

I pulled the car onto 82nd Street and could barely see the red taillights of the cars in front of me. The rain got harder. Charlie cried louder.

"Can I give him some of my candy, Momma?" Willie offered.

"No, he's still too young to have candy," I said.

"It's okay, Char. We'll be home soon," Lucy cooed to him.

For the next fifteen minutes, we barely moved. I turned on the heat in the car seats to try and warm up. Willie and Lucy continued to try and cheer up Charlie with no luck. Finally they got tired too.

"We'll be home soon," I said as I took a right turn to try another route. I continued to slowly navigate the dark, congested roads. I made it to Fall Creek Road hoping the traffic would be better. It had now been forty-five minutes since we left the mall. We all wanted out of the car to get away from Charlie's cries. My breasts filled with milk. I squeezed my chest to stop the milk from flowing through my shirt.

"I'm hungry," Willie said.

"I have to go to the bathroom," Sam said.

"I'm thirsty," Lucy said.

The two-lane road was slick from the freezing rain. As I was going around a curve, I reached forward and turned on the radio—and there he was.

Paul singing "Hey Jude."

I took a deep breath into my frozen body. By the end of the first verse, the car was silent. Charlie had stopped crying, and now I was the one with the tears.

Sam, peeking over at me, started singing the chorus with Paul, John, Ringo and George. Lucy joined in. Then Willie.

We all sang.

The song was seven minutes. We made it home not too long after it ended. We were hungry and tired, but the music had begun to thaw the chill of the night. Ben was waiting for us with dinner and warm towels. We dried off and ate dinner together like maybe there was hope for something better for the future of our marriage and for the future of our family.

Many years after Ben and I divorced, I read that Paul McCartney wrote "Hey Jude" for John Lennon's son, Julian, to cheer him up during his parents' divorce. It was "Hey Jules" at first, but Paul liked the sound of "Hey Jude." I wished I could have written a song or a poem that helped my children through our divorce. I wished there was something we could sing together now, to bring us back to love, back to that moment in the car where everything was better.

In May of 2016, the month after he turned twenty-three, my son Willie had a seizure and nearly died in my arms. It was during his sister Lucy's graduation weekend in Austin, Texas. Lucy was getting her master's degree in education. Ben had come to Austin to join Sam, Willie, Lucy, and me for a weekend of festivities. Charlie, our youngest, was unable to attend. It was going to be the first time in eight months that I'd be with most of my children. The four children, all in their twenties, now lived in four states and I didn't have a home anymore for them to come visit.

Ahead of the weekend, Lucy sent a group text informing us of the planned activities—dinner and game night at her house, swimming in a natural springs swimming pool under the full moon, and a brunch where we would all contribute a dish. She added that she had a code word to be said if conversations got heated—it hadn't been easy for any of us since Ben became involved with Annie. It would be the first time in several years that Ben, the kids, and I shared meals together. Lucy text us that the code word was "Elsa," with the reminder of the song Elsa sings in the movie *Frozen*: "Let It Go." I smiled knowing how much this weekend meant to Lucy and how much she wanted it to be healing for our family.

The first days of the trip were fantastic. I arrived early and enjoyed time with Lucy. When Sam and Willie arrived, we sat outside at one of Austin's cool restaurants and shared drinks, burgers, fries, and laughter. Ben was arriving the next day, so I was happy to have them all to myself and share our first meal and conversation together.

The next morning Sam slept in while Lucy, Willie, and I went to breakfast. It was a warm spring day, and we chose to sit outside and have tacos at a popular breakfast spot. I sat by myself for a few minutes while Lucy and Willie went in to order. I closed my eyes and let the sun kiss my skin.

After they ordered, Willie, a Chicago-based comedian, took the seat next to me.

"What's up, Big Momma?" he playfully asked as he sat down. Willie gave everyone nicknames. I wasn't thrilled about mine.

Our breakfast arrived, and even though we had drinks, he asked Lucy to get him water.

"I'm so thirsty," I heard him say, and then I turned to him, and his face and body were suddenly grotesquely contorted. At first, I thought he was making a joke and then realized there was blood running out of his mouth. It appeared that he was biting his tongue off as his body shook violently.

My daughter Lucy stood up almost robotically and said, "I know what this is; he's having a seizure."

All sounds faded in the background as I got behind him and pulled his 6'1" body out of his chair. With the help of strangers, we put him on his side with me under him, cradling his head so it wouldn't hit the cement. Even though I knew I shouldn't, I tried to stick my fingers in his mouth to pry his teeth off his bleeding tongue. His jaw was locked, and bloody white foam ran from the edges of his mouth and onto my fingers.

Suddenly his face turned pale, and his body went limp.

My Willie. My sweet Willie.

Please come back, Willie, was my silent prayer.

I remember locking eyes with a woman at the table next to us, needing hope in that moment. Her eyes sent back love. It felt like everyone around us was.

"He's going to be okay," I heard. A man knelt down next to me. His voice was soft but confident. He mentioned he was an ER nurse.

"Most likely this is a grand mal seizure," he continued. "Don't put anything in his mouth."

Suddenly, Willie started shaking violently—his arms and legs writhed as color began to return to his cheeks.

It was mesmerizing to watch the body in shock when nothing was communicating the right messages. His mouth was still locked into an odd shape. I cradled his head thinking, *Please remember what you are supposed to do. Your body knows how to heal, Willie.*

"Keep him on his side."

"Don't ask him questions."

"Speak softly and calmly."

I looked up at Lucy on the phone with emergency services. She was supposed to be graduating in twenty-four hours. An ambulance arrived, and Willie was taken to the ER.

I knew he had been sad about the suicide of his college roommate two years earlier. Could he have been self-medicating? It was one moment that I hoped that it was a drug problem, not a problem with his brain, or a disease.

After tests came back, the doctor suggested it was caused by "the perfect storm of alcohol, Xanax withdrawals, and dehydration." The doctor released him saying, "First seizure, you get a pass." The doctor didn't make a big deal about it so we didn't either. It was good to get him released from the hospital. Willie said he'd make better choices.

We went home to the condo we were sharing for the weekend and put Willie to bed so he could rest. Two hours later, Ben arrived, and as Willie got up to tell him about the seizure, he started to spin. Ben and I caught our son, and we all fell to the ground. We ended up back in the ER and then Willie was admitted for a detox. The Xanax abuse had been more serious. He'd been medicating the sadness and staying silent. I spent that night with Willie at the hospital and then left the next morning at 7:00 to meet Lucy for her graduation at 9:00. I knew what this day and this weekend meant to her.

With Willie recovering in the hospital, we celebrated Lucy's graduation with brunch afterwards. Walking into the restaurant, Ben asked everyone but me to stand in front of the restaurant sign. I wasn't to be included in *his* family photo. During the meal, he repeatedly interrupted me, talking over me like my voice didn't matter. I looked at Lucy who already knew the weekend wasn't about her anymore.

Elsa, I thought. *Let it go.*

"God has got you covered," a man said in a thick Texas accent.

That statement came later that night from a man at a chic new restaurant in Austin. Our table wasn't ready, so I went to get drinks for everyone. I stood next to a man who was finishing dinner at the bar.

"Let me buy you a drink," he said.

"I'm good, thanks," I said, not in the mood to engage. "And I'm getting seven drinks. I'm here with my family."

"Then let me buy you seven drinks," he replied. My body absorbed his words like I had been dehydrated from lack of water, lack of life. I drank in his words like an elixir and just for one moment, I remembered I was a woman again, one who longed to be appreciated.

"Thank you," I said. "If you only knew my past twenty-four hours."

"She needs seven drinks," he said to the bartender. "Put them on my tab."

I could feel the pressure of tears coming into my eyes. I didn't try to blink them away.

"Thank you." I was surprised I was able to smile as I said it. "My daughter graduated today. She got her master's degree." I stopped speaking before anymore of the story came out.

"My name is Nikolai," he said. "Order your seven drinks and choose two bottles of wine, and I'll send them to your table for dinner."

I asked him why. He said, "I just want you to know God has got you covered."

The seven drinks came. I didn't want to leave him. Or I wanted to take him to our table so I had someone on my side. I thanked him again.

"Don't ever forget," Nikolai said. "God has got you covered."

That night I let myself get a little bit drunk, but not as a way to numb any pain. I toasted to celebrate Lucy. I toasted to celebrate all the moments of the weekend as I remembered that life isn't just about the sad moments or the happy moments; life is about all of the moments. Like Paul says in "Hey Jude," even the sad ones will get better.

The next morning, with Willie still in the hospital, Ben left for the airport at 6:00. He said he had to get back to his work; he had important meetings the next day. He didn't bother to ask me what my plans were.

I had planned on flying out the same day to complete a certification course I was taking in Somatic Bodywork, something that was important to the work and writing I was doing. With Willie in the hospital, I changed plans to stay in Austin until he was discharged. I dropped Sam, who also had to head home, at the airport and then went to visit Willie. He was looking more like himself, but it was hard to shake the vision of his gnarled face and body during his seizures. Every time I had tried to sleep during the past two nights, the scene would repeat itself. I would open my eyes to make it go away.

I was exhausted. I hadn't slept much or bathed in the past forty-eight hours. Lucy was asleep at her apartment, and I didn't want to wake her. After our family dinner, she'd spent the night celebrating her graduation with her class.

I decided to get a hotel room so I could at least take a shower and sleep for a few hours.

"I'm sorry, we're fully booked," was the response at the first hotel. "It's graduation weekend."

I sat in my rental car for thirty minutes with both my mind and the car engine running. What had happened to the weekend? What had happened to my family? There wasn't enough juice in my body to create any tears.

It felt like a small miracle when I got a room at the second hotel I tried. It was nearby, so I drove straight there. I didn't bother to get my luggage out of the car. I only wanted to take a shower and sleep. It was one in the afternoon.

"How was your weekend?" the girl asked at check-in. She was about my daughter's age and had a smile like a Disney princess.

I smiled, unable to answer her question. I was afraid a swell of anguish would be released if my lips parted further.

"Were you here for graduation?"

I nodded my head.

"Congratulations! You must be so proud."

I nodded again, thinking back to the moment the day before when Lucy walked across the stage and received her certificate. She was going to be a high-school teacher. And this was my child who never liked to go to school when she was younger. Now, she was passionate about being an advocate for students to learn in a safe and engaging environment where all their voices mattered.

The girl checking me in reached across the desk and handed me a bottle of water and a room key. "If you need anything, my name is Elsa. I wrote it down so you won't forget."

Elsa.

I couldn't believe it.

Yes, I remembered. *Let it go.*

Two days later, Willie was released from the hospital. We drove straight to the airport. As we pulled in, "Hey Jude" came on the radio. I reached over and turned up the volume.

TWENTY

My early summer plans changed so I could stay closer to Chicago and take Willie to appointments to get evaluated. I had to ask Ben for extra money to help me live through this period, as I was unable to work. He rarely responded to my texts and just had his assistant put the money in my account.

In the coming months, I lived and worked between homes and beds in Chicago, Sacramento, Dallas, Austin, New York City, Miami, Australia (again), France, and London. I was never in any place for long—sometimes a few days, sometimes a few weeks. When I had privacy, I continued to do my bliss sessions. Even when I missed a few days, I still noticed when I took a deep conscious breath my spine tingled with ecstasy, my genitals fluttered, and my skin got chills as the neural pathways lit up like holiday lights. It was as if my entire essence was activated by the months of self-care. I realized I'd transformed from living in a numb, frozen state that occurs with trauma to an awakened and animated state. Even as I was dealing with challenges in life, my body was still choosing to coexist in a state of wellness and joy.

The second volume of *Autobiographies of Our Orgasms* was released that summer. The first O anthology had a black O on the cover. The second book had a blood red O on the cover and featured stories by sixteen women from the US and Australia. Over the past year, I witnessed the metamorphosis in the women who wrote stories for the first book. Writing the truth about their sensual paths enabled them to create autonomy and ownership over their bodies, especially for the ones who had experienced abuse. Their writing was medicine for their healing.

I also felt my voice growing stronger. During one of my bodywork sessions, I spent over hour slowly massaging myself, allowing the energy between my fingers and my skin to guide my touch. My head tilted back and my mouth dropped open as I traced circles around my throat, an area that I had always wanted to protect before, sometimes actually feeling that it had been slit when I used my voice. *Where did that memory come from?* Now the tenderness of my touch created a safety net for speaking up. I tended to my neck in the same way an athlete might gently stretch her body before an event. I noticed as I rubbed my throat, my pelvic area also softened, and a deep low hum was released from within. I remembered giving birth to my children and being encouraged to take an epidural so I wouldn't feel a thing. I wondered what I missed out on during the four births by not allowing my voice and my hips to be in sync with bringing my children into the world.

I was content to be living out in the world with a body that was healed. A few people mentioned that I looked younger. "What are you doing?" they asked, maybe thinking it was a new skin care product I was using. "It's a beauty tonic called orgasm," I wanted to say; however it wasn't just about the orgasm, it was that I'd made the choice to nurture my sensual energy and it went beyond the orgasm. The hormones released by choosing to feel good in my body were an elixir for good health.

While I was still committed to nourishing my own sensual energy, I was also open to meeting a man. That moment in the restaurant with Nikolai was the first time in a long time that I'd felt seen by a man, and it was in a moment of vulnerability.

The last relationship I had was over five years before, and it was brief. I'd healed my body but realized my heart was not healed or at least had been closed for a long, long time. How do you open a closed heart?

I was fifty-three and for the first time felt ready to let someone in. I was seeing many of my closest friends discovering love after waiting for the *right* one. Love seemed to be all around me, so I was stunned when I read Elizabeth Gilbert's Facebook post on July 1, 2016, where she announced she was divorcing "Felipe," the man she met at the end of her book *Eat, Pray, Love*. How could that love story end? That book gave so many of us hope for a love story with a beloved, especially when we follow our heart. A few months later, Elizabeth announced she'd begun a same-sex relationship with her best friend, Rayya Elias, the same woman I'd met with her in Byron Bay the year before. It made me happy to see people following their hearts. Love is love. I was ready for it however it wanted to show up.

By the end of the summer, I was still living without a home. It had been almost two years. I was not making enough income to buy or rent a home, however I was finding ways to live around the world as I hosted workshops and retreats. I was living my own version of *Eat, Pray, Love* but the love affair was with myself.

I was content seeing my children happy and engaged in work they loved. My son Sam was a key part of the thriving Indianapolis comedy scene, and he also played bass in a local band. Lucy was starting her first year teaching high school in Austin, Texas. Willie was immersed in the Chicago comedy scene and even making the choice to talk about his drug use, the death of close friends to drugs, and his own body's warning of having a seizure to make him pay attention to his choices. Our bodies are always giving us messages. I was glad that Willie was finally listening. Some of the best news came from my youngest son, Charlie, who announced that his partner Harley was expecting their first child. I was going to be a grandmother.

TWENTY-ONE

With the exception of the ten years I was married, I've spent all of my life looking for a place to call home.

My gypsy life started early. Up until 2014, I always had a home, but I was also living between homes, never fully settling in. Even during my ten years of marriage, we moved four different times; it seemed we were always in the middle of remodeling or building every time I was pregnant. I gave birth to four children in five years. We moved four times in ten years. I was always packing and unpacking. After my divorce, when I moved to Miami, I unpacked the children's rooms, but most of my things stayed packed in boxes in the garage.

I've lived out of a suitcase for most of my life. The vagabond life chose me the day I was born. My parents already had three children, two girls and a boy, so with my birth, they weren't hoping for anything. My mom later told me, "You were an accident."

On February 2, 1963, false contractions sent my mom to the hospital. My dad, Richard, had been stocking the shelves of our family-run grocery store, Richard's Market Basket, when he got the call to come home and drive Mom to the hospital. Several hours later, the contractions stopped, and my parents returned home. They were too tired to notice the red spots popping up on my sister Susan. By the time I was born three days later, they knew that my siblings Sharon and David would also get the chicken pox.

My mom gave birth to me just before lunch on February 5th. I was named Betty Jane after a close friend of my parents—Betty Anshutz. Betty and her husband Bill were asked be my godparents.

Betty and Bill offered to take me to their house and care for me until my siblings were better. My parents didn't protest, especially since their home shared a backyard divided by a fence with my godparents' home. Two days later, my mom went home to my dad and my sick siblings, and I went home with Betty and Bill. Their teenage daughters, Wendy and Cathy, were waiting on the front porch to meet me. I can imagine myself smiling up at the four of them gazing at me reverently while I'm thinking, *Now this is more like it.*

After two weeks, my mom tried to take me home, but Betty, a nurse, and Bill, a doctor, who'd both served during the war, inspected the nearly healed chicken pox on my siblings and told Mom, "We better keep the baby a few more weeks just to be safe," like it was a war zone at the Blankenbaker house.

I always wondered how it was so easy for my mom to give me away when I was born. Did she not want to bond with me or nurse me or spend the first moments of my life with me? I always felt like an outsider in my own family.

Later I found out that Betty's third child was a girl named Judy whom she delivered stillborn at full term. Betty was put to sleep for the delivery, expecting to hold her third child after the procedure. Instead, when she woke up, she found out her baby was dead. She was so upset, she refused to see her.

Betty held Judy only in her womb, never in her arms. Eight years after she chose not to hold her dead baby, I was placed in Betty's arms. "After you were born and named after Mom, she felt like she got another chance to be a mother," my godsister Cathy told me. "You were the reason my parents were able to move forward after losing Judy."

I stayed with my godparents for several weeks until my mom finally walked through the backyard gate to bring home. In many ways, I never left the Anshutz home. I spent as much time with them during my childhood as I did my own family.

My godsister Cathy told me, "You were the sparkling gem of our family. You brought joy to everyone in the family. As a matter of fact, Wendy and I would both agree that you were the favorite daughter. This never caused us any grief because we too adored you. You brought Mom and Dad immeasurable joy."

Once home, my siblings pronounced my name Betsy instead of Betty, so not only did I change homes, I also changed names.

There were two kids' bedrooms at the Blankenbaker home. Susan and Sharon shared the girls' room, and my crib shared a room with my brother David. Even after I left their home, Wendy or Cathy would get off the school bus every day on my parents' street, check on me to make sure I didn't need a bottle or clean diaper, pick me up, and with my mom's permission, walk through the backyard to their home, where I would stay for a few hours. Wendy said, "I didn't notice that you ever left. You stayed in our hearts."

As soon as I could crawl, I would head towards the gate to Betty's house. And then I walked there. My brothers and sisters rarely followed me. Betty's house was my place. Once I crossed that gate, I went from being from an accidental pregnancy to being a gift for my godparents.

The following November of 1964, Mom gave birth to my little brother Jim. That same year she won an award for being the 1964 Day Nursery Volunteer of the Year. Day Nursery was an organization devoted to providing early childhood education and childcare for families in need. In 1964, Mom had four children at home under the age of seven, a baby on the way, AND she won an award for taking care of other people's children. We were not surprised when she ran for public office later in life. She was always finding ways to make a difference.

When I was three, my parents found a bigger home six miles from Betty and Bill's house. We moved from the suburbs to an affordable old colonial house closer to the city and three times the size of our previous home.

Betty taught me how to use the phone to call her. The phone had two parts, a handset that you put to your ear to talk and a base that had numbers and a circular dial. I would press my small fingers into the circle over each number and tug at the plastic dial. We practiced until I memorized the numbers. After we moved, Betty locked the backyard gate between the houses.

At my new home, we all got our own rooms. I had one of the smallest rooms with two doors that locked. I loved having my own space. It was in that childhood bedroom, the first room I had to myself, that an older neighbor molested me when I was six.

I wrote about that moment in *Autobiography of an Orgasm*:

Moving into the bigger house meant I no longer had to share a bedroom with my brothers; I finally had my own room, and I loved it. My mom had covered one wall with scenes from my favorite book, Snow White and the Seven Dwarfs. *I can still remember looking at that wallpaper while my neighbor was molesting me. I was six.*

It was a beautiful summer day when Val, a teenage neighbor, invited me to play. She said we needed to use one of our bedrooms. The four homes around us had families with lots of kids, so I guess it wasn't strange to my mom to see me come into the house with an older girl. Val was seven years older than me, closer to my oldest sister's age. I liked the attention from an older friend. She told me to lie down on my bed. We were going to play doctor.

"Take off your shorts. I need to check you."

I had never played doctor before, but I did as I was told. I pushed my shorts down to my knees.

"Take off your underwear too," she said.

I didn't know the rules. I pushed my underwear down, even though I remembered my godfather was a real doctor, and he never asked me to remove my underwear.

I felt a tickle as she glided her fingers across my belly. I had been in a swimming pool earlier in the day, and I watched her fingers leaving tracks on my dry skin.

"Open your legs," she said. I opened them as wide as my underwear and shorts around my knees would allow. She rubbed my thighs and then up to the place where pee came out of me. I didn't know what to call it. I felt butterflies in my belly when she touched me. It felt good. I didn't want to look at her, so I turned my head and looked at the wallpaper. Snow White was inches from my face, smiling at me.

Suddenly, it felt like she was tearing me apart. Her fingers were inside me. She put her other hand on my mouth. "Say nothing," she said. She didn't sound like my friend anymore. I held my breath and tightened my legs, hoping to squeeze her out of me.

(Excerpted from *Autobiography of an Orgasm*)

Like many times in my childhood, I called Betty to come pick up that day, and I stayed at their house that night. I didn't tell them what had happened, but I felt safe at their home. I didn't realize that by running from my home, the memory was still stored in my body, and it stayed there for nearly fifty years until I stopped running and made the choice to heal.

One thing about remembering is that you question your memory. What is the truth? What really happened? How can I trust my memory, especially after so long? As I remembered, I recalled that day through the sensory memories. I'd been swimming and could smell the dried chlorine on my skin. I could feel the neighbor tracing her fingers up my suntanned legs and over my butt. I could see the scenes of Snow White on the wallpaper as I turned my head away from the teenager fondling me. My bedroom window was open, and I could hear the neighbors still swimming next door. I wondered, why I didn't scream?

From that day forward, I often had tonsillitis or strep throat. I'd always call my godparents, and Bill would rush to my house while Betty made a sick bed for me on their sofa. She'd set up a dinner tray next to me with a glass of 7-Up and a small bell to ring if I needed anything. Bill made me gargle with salt water, and then he'd check my heart with his stethoscope before he gave me a shot of penicillin. When I asked what my heart sounded like, Bill put the ear buds of his stethoscope to my ears. *Swoosh, swoosh. Swoosh, swoosh,* I heard. Then he moved the scope to his own heart. I called my godmother into the room so I could hear her heart. We all sounded the same.

I never told my godparents what happened that day, but throughout my life their home was a sanctuary for me.

Betty and Bill were in their late sixties when my first child, Sam, was born. He started going to their house for visits when he was a baby. I watched Sam fall in love with Betty for all the same reasons I had. She showed him where to dig for worms and taught him how to hammer nails. Sam hid with Betty in the front yard bushes just like I had, hunting for imaginary bears with a fake shotgun. When he could stand, Sam stood at Bill's side as he played his treasured Steinway piano. Sam swayed to the music as he watched Bill's hands glide over the keys.

After Bill died, I invited Betty to spend more time with my family at our home, but she preferred to watch one or two of my children at her house. When I was pregnant with my fourth child, we had moved into our fourth house in six years—a 10,000-square-foot home we built bordering a lake. One time when Betty came to babysit, I found her sitting on the floor outside Willie's room as he napped. He was two. She'd been there for almost two hours. When I asked her why she didn't wait downstairs for him to wake up, she said the house was so big she'd was afraid she wouldn't be able to find his room again.

When Sam was six, I invited Betty to fly with me to a resort in Phoenix for a weekend trip. We took Sam and my fourth child, Charlie, who was six months old. Betty sat by the resort pool with Charlie and watched Sam swim while I went for a hike or took a yoga class. A few days into the trip, we decided to drive to the Grand Canyon, which was six to seven hours round trip. I was still nursing Charlie, so it wasn't a drive I desired to make, but in her seventy-two years Betty had never asked me to do anything; she had only given to me. "I've never seen the Grand Canyon," she said. I knew I had to take her there.

When we arrived, we had a short walk to the canyon rim. I took Charlie from Betty after I noticed her breathing harder. Sam took Betty's hand and continued to the top of the trail. When we got to the edge of the canyon, Betty and I stood with the boys and gazed out at the immense hole in the land. She said, "I've seen the Grand Canyon; now I can die."

A few months after we returned from Phoenix, Betty said it was bothering her that she was getting short of breath when she played with my kids. The doctor ran tests and told her she had some blockage in the veins pumping blood into her heart. He said she would eventually need surgery, but there was no rush. He advised her to slow down and to avoid doing the things that caused her shortness of breath, like playing ball with my four kids in her backyard. Instead, Betty decided to do the surgery right away. "I want to be able to keep up with your kids," she told me.

I asked her what she wanted for her seventy-third birthday.

"One of those inflatable houses you got for your kids' birthdays," she replied.

"A bounce-house?" I said.

"Yes, and let's order pizza and cake and invite the neighborhood kids."

On May 18th, Betty celebrated her birthday with a clown bounce-house set up in her driveway. When the company delivered it, the men asked, "How old is the birthday girl?"

"Seventy-three," Betty replied. They smiled and told her she could keep it for an extra day.

Two months later, Sam stayed with Betty the night before she checked into the hospital. She set up tray tables with their dinner in front of the couch, and they watched TV together before they read books and went to bed. When I picked Sam up the next day, Betty told him she would play ball with him again after the doctor fixed her heart. She never came home. She died of an infection she most likely got during surgery.

My godsisters Wendy and Cathy joined me for the funeral. It had been almost five years since the three of us were together for the funeral of their father and my godfather, Bill.

Betty died July 28, 1996. After her death, I learned that her given name was Eliza Jane. A few years before Betty died, she had her name legally changed to Betty Jane because of how I had always signed cards to her throughout my life. *To: Betty Jane I, Love from Betty Jane II.* When the judge asked her why at age seventy she wanted to legally change her name, she told him, "Because my goddaughter was named after me, and I want us to have the same names." He approved the name change and told

Betty in all his years working as a judge that was the best reason he'd ever heard for a name change.

Betty's house was packed up and sold after her death. It was my first home, and now it—and she—were gone. As my godsisters packed the house, they found a small, red, round suitcase in Betty's closet. It was my first piece of luggage, just big enough for a three-year-old to carry when I moved to my new house. It was filled with cards, letters, and art that I had giving to Betty and Bill over the years.

It took fifty-three years for me to understand the truth about my birth. I had always wondered why I was always looking for my home in the world, and I think it started with not going home at birth—which was one of the biggest gifts of my life.

In 2016, I was asked to write a story for my friend Jaime Fleres' book, *Birth Your Story: Why Writing About Your Birth Matters.* I had intended to write about giving birth for the first time, but the writing process is always revealing, and while I did write about Sam's birth, I also recalled my own birth. I finally realized the sacrifice my mother made during the early weeks of my life—her heart was big enough to offer her newborn to another mother who never got to hold her own.

TWENTY-TWO

If ten years ago a psychic had told me my former husband would be in a relationship with our former babysitter or that I, at the age of fifty-four, would be living without a home base, I would have asked the psychic for my money back.

If she told me I'd write a book on orgasms, I would have rolled my eyes. I would have also told the psychic she was not very intuitive if she suggested someday I'd bury a baby in Zimbabwe or get up on stage in front of 300 people and talk about my sensuality. If she told me in my fifties, I'd be teaching dance around the world, I'd shake my head no, that would never happen. After all, when I was eight, I overheard my ballet teacher tell my mom to put me in something else. "She's not a dancer," he said in a thick Russian accent.

But it all happened—and more—and parts of the story were so painful to live that the only thing that made sense was when a friend told me something else I didn't want to hear: "Imagine your old life has been hit by a nuclear bomb," Sarah said. "It's gone. Walk away from the ashes."

151

No, I can heal my family, I thought. *My family is my life.* But I knew Sarah was right, the version of my family I gave birth to and nurtured, both before and after my divorce, was blown apart after Ben became involved with Annie. In the midst of the explosion, I also felt that someday my children and I might look back on this ending as the beginning of something better.

In January of 2017, during a visit to my birthplace, Indianapolis, I was saying to a friend, "You know the Hafiz poem about God circling the place you are right now as where you are supposed to be?"

She nodded yes.

"I just can't believe God wants me in this place right now. I'm about to be a grandmother to the same baby as my old babysitter. Annie won't even speak to me and we used to be friends. I trusted her. "

Less than twelve hours after I mentioned the Hafiz quote to my friend, I passed by a restaurant to get a tea on the way to the airport. Once again, I was leaving Indiana after a visit to see two of my children for a belated Christmas celebration. It was a busy Sunday morning in the restaurant. There was not much space to move as I waited for my order. I stood to the side of the woman at the front of the line but didn't see her face until she turned around. It was Annie. She turned away from me without saying anything. We stood there, inches from each other without saying a word. Finally, I said, "God has a sense of humor."

"Stop being a victim of your own life," she replied, her eyes and words filled with hate.

My body shook as I left the restaurant, wondering why did I have to have the encounter. And then I remembered the line she said to me was similar to one I wrote in my book, *Autobiography of an Orgasm*. She claimed my words, and it felt like she claimed my former life.

The next day morning as I took a walk in Los Angeles, I listened to a recording from a favorite writer, Tosha Silver. She started the call with the same Hafiz quote:

"The place where you are right now God circled on a map for you."

You've got to be kidding. Is this synchronicity? What was the message?

That night I'd had a disturbing dream of Annie trying to choke me. I was flying onward to Kauai the next day, and on the way to the Los Angeles airport, I said a prayer.

Please release me from feeling hurt, angry, betrayed. Please change me into someone who accepts the situation as part of a bigger plan, and show me the way to release the pain.

As I pulled into the Hertz car rental parking lot, the sun was rising and beginning to light up Los Angeles. I was glad for a moment I wasn't too busy in my head to notice the arch of light as it announced the beginning of a new day. And just like the opening of a good movie, every Hertz worker was smiling, backlit by the tangerine sky. Everyone looked as if they were dancing through the morning sunlight.

"Good morning!" one said.

"Can I help carry anything?" another said.

"Have a good day!" another one added.

I missed the first Hertz shuttle bus to take me to the airport. It pulled away just as I walked up to board. *Can't the driver see me?*

When the next bus pulled up, the doors opened. I saw the driver, a woman close to my age, in an over-sized Hertz shirt and pants. She unbuckled her seat belt and walked towards me to help with the luggage. I took a seat and started to check my phone for messages and to scroll through social networking.

"Welcome to another day in paradise," I heard the driver say. She wasn't joking. Her words inspired me to put my phone into my bag; I watched her light up everyone's mood with her kindness and smile.

After everyone was loaded on the bus, she drove us to the airport, dropping people off one by one. At the end, it was just the two of us. "My name is Beautiful," she said. She laughed as we talked about our children and my soon-to-be grandchild. "What's your grandmother name going to be?" she asked.

In that instant, I proclaimed, "GoGo. It means Grandmother in Shona, the indigenous language of Zimbabwe," I said. "I spend several weeks every year in Zimbabwe. It's one of the places that feel like home."

"GoGo," she smiled as she looked at me in her rearview mirror. "There is no one like you."

And in that moment, the spell of the old story was broken. I could feel the heaviness of the past five years melt from my body. I was living in the moment and not in the past. I was living in the place God had circled for me that day. And it was Beautiful.

TWENTY-THREE

I woke up in Bali earlier than usual on March 4, 2017 to a dream that Harley was screaming, but it wasn't from a place of being scared, it was more like a roar of a lioness protecting her young. I looked at my watch; it was late afternoon in California where my son Charlie and Harley lived. The baby wasn't due for another week.

I texted Charlie, "How is Harley?"

A few minutes later, he wrote, "You're a grandma" and sent a photo of her holding a baby. She'd just given birth and was still in the bath she'd delivered in. Her face held joy, pain, power, and relief in the same expression. In all my deliveries, there had been no screaming—all the drugs I'd been offered took the edge off. I stared at the photo, grateful for this woman choosing to bring my grandchild into the world where the first thing she heard was her mom's voice, a howl welcoming her into the lineage of women who were ready to be heard.

Six weeks after my granddaughter was brought in with a wail, I was using my voice in bigger ways too. The event was called the

Walk the Talk Series, a TED Talk-inspired series in my hometown of Indianapolis. I was one of the selected speakers. The theme of the evening was Positive Thinking. I would be the last to speak.

The Vogue Theater was packed with nearly 300 people. I was nervous to reveal so much not just in front of my conservative hometown but also because my mother was coming to the event. While I knew most of the speakers would be taking a traditional approach to a speech on positive thinking, I decided to offer my experience of orgasm as being positive thinking for the body, and maybe we should be focused on positive feeling instead.

I was going to talk transparently about the effects of sexual assault on the body, about faking it, about my five years of research, and about becoming the sensual expert on my body. I was also hoping to make people laugh, even though the topic was a serious one. Just before I went on stage, my son Willie texted me from Chicago.

"Don't try to be funny," he wrote. "Just tell your story."

The butterflies rose in my stomach as my name was announced. As I walked on stage, I wasn't too sure I even remembered my first line. It got quiet in the theater as my eyes tried to adjust to the bright stage lights shining at me. I looked at the crowd. I took time to make eye contact with some people I knew sitting in the front row – Vicki, Jodi, Iva. Off to my right, I could see my mom sitting with her book club friends, Lottie and

Beth. I wondered what she would think of my talk. I knew I wasn't living the life she wanted for me. I opened my mouth and spoke:

"I'm born and raised in Indianapolis.

On the one occasion I can remember Mom talking to me about my genitals, she simply pointed and softly whispered, 'down there.'

She was shocked when I released a book called Autobiography of an Orgasm.

My book is about the five years I spent researching orgasm as a way to heal my body after sexual assault.

When my book came out, Mom chose not to read it. I understand.

She's here tonight.

I looked over at mom and her friends again. Mom was used to being seen, but I'm sure this was not her ideal introduction.

"My mom is State Senator Virginia Blankenbaker. She retired in 1992 after serving for twelve years. Some of you may not have seen her since then. I asked her to send a photo in case you didn't recognize her—and also told her I'd be talking about my book. This is the photo she sent.

On a large screen behind me a photo of a woman with a bag over her head appeared.

"I guess she still doesn't want to talk about orgasm.

I heard laughter. I tried to continue, but the audience was still laughing. I looked over at Mom, and she was smiling. *Everything is okay*, I thought. I continued:

"When I told Mom about my book she said, 'but we don't talk about those things.'

And I could hear her mother and her grandmother and generations of women in my family and in your families saying the same thing. We don't talk about those things.

Being positive—does it mean only speaking happy words, or does it mean speaking what is true?

The audience was still. I looked at my friend Iva. She was sitting in the front row with her mother who was the same generation as my mother. I know they had come to listen to talks on positive thinking, not orgasm.

"So what does orgasm have to do with positive thinking?

Positive thinking is using language and thought to bring more good into your life.

But what if instead of positive thinking, we choose positive feeling?

Orgasm is a natural way to bring more good feelings into your body.

Orgasm is positive thinking—for the body.

We don't say no, no, no during orgasm.

We say yes, yes, yes.

More laughter. I smiled knowing I was breaking years of silence in the lineage of women in my family. When it got quiet, I went on:

"For more than half my life, I was saying yes, yes, yes, but I was feeling nothing. I was smiling and faking it.

My mom knows the risks of speaking up.

In 1992, her child-support bill put in place requirements for the so-called deadbeat dads to pay child support, or their wages would be garnished. That night, a bullet was fired through my mom's bedroom window—it landed just above where she was sleeping.

But Mom continued to take a stand for the marginalized voices, especially women, children, and the elderly. And tonight, I'd like to tell you about a marginalized voice that I took a stand for—my vagina.

By the time I was forty, I could tell you all the words to my ten favorite songs, I could tell you in detail how to make my favorite dinner, I could tell you how to jump a dead battery on your car. I couldn't tell you how to give me an orgasm.

One in three women in this room will experience abuse against their bodies during their lifetime, for more than half, like me, it will be before the age of eighteen. It may be physical; it may be emotional or verbal. And most of us stay quiet because . . . we don't talk about those things.

About one in three women in this room would also be clinically be diagnosed with female sexual dysfunction. They don't feel good in their bodies—even though it's a birthright.

When the body experiences trauma, it stores the information, and unless we re-train the body with new information and bring the body back into balance, the body will continue to be in a fight-or-flight mode. The damage can go on for years with the effects showing up as sickness, depression, and other diseases.

I was numb. I was not feeling my orgasm. I was not feeling my life.

For forty years, I was always sick with the flu and sore throats. I was told I was depressed. A doctor gave me Prozac.

It made me wonder, was I depressed, or maybe my vagina was depressed? Did the sore throats have anything to do with me not speaking up?

I went to doctors and therapists who told me what was wrong with me until one day I decided to figure out what was right with me.

I looked over at Mom, but I couldn't see her through the bright lights. I hoped she was still doing okay with the talk. I kept speaking:

"Almost ten years ago, at the age of forty-five, I took myself on as a research project to see if I could feel my orgasm after a lifetime of feeling nothing. Remember, I had never told anyone about the damage I experienced, so I also didn't tell anyone about the research. It was embarrassing to me, so I kept it a secret.

To start my research, I simply Googled videos on how to have an orgasm.

More giggles.

I do not advise you do that.

My body softened. I felt lighter. I remembered the theater where I was speaking was one of the places I came on a first date with Ben. I smiled and continued:

"The next thing I did was read books called

Easy Orgasm

The Elusive Orgasm

Extended Orgasm

Extended Massive Orgasm

Instant Orgasm

Real Orgasm

Tantric Orgasm

Super Orgasm

And I even followed the advice in the Multi-Orgasmic Diet.

I started to look for courses. Maybe that would help.

I was living in Indiana and didn't bother to look for courses here—I would be too embarrassed to show up in a group: Hi, I'm Betsy and I'm trying to find my orgasm.

I wanted to do this research anonymously, so when I dropped my son Sam off at his first week of college in New York City, I signed up for a course on orgasm. No one would know me in New York.

I'd been a swimmer when I was younger, so I understood that I could train my body.

I decided to quietly take up orgasm as my sport. I just had no idea if I'd be any good.

I signed up for a course to find my orgasm only to discover there is more than one kind.

One course guaranteed the secrets to four types of orgasm.

Another said nine.

Another expert told me there were seventy types of orgasm.

I was just looking for one.

I could see my mom's face turning bright red from laughing. I am finally getting to have the sex talk with her, but with a twist.

"I want to tell you a little more about my research, but I want my mom to be comfortable—remember, she hasn't read my book.

To make her more comfortable, I'd like to use code words. And since it's almost the month of May, let's compare my genitals with the Indy 500 racetrack.

A large oval appears on the screen behind me with the shorter ends of the oval at the bottom and top of the screen. This is Indiana so it's likely nearly every person in the room has been to the Indy 500 race at least once in their lives.

"Here's the track: imagine that the racetrack represents the vulva.

The room of nearly three hundred erupts in chuckles.

"The interior of the track, the infield, is the vagina,

And this spot up at the top, the pit stop, is the clitoris.

A small black dot appears at the top of the oval.

"So basically, I was working with sex experts in New York City who were advising me on how much time to spend on the racetrack, or in the infield, or how often to visit the pit stop. I was looking for some combination that would help me orgasm, or I guess win the race.

One course, called Orgasmic Meditation, taught me that maybe I want to spend the whole race in the pit stop.

One sex expert advised me to spend more time in the infield but not all the way in—there is supposed to be a special party place in the infield called the G spot.

To strengthen my infield, I took a course on how to hold a jade egg inside my vagina, I mean the infield.

The egg, carved from jade, is about the size of an egg you'd eat for breakfast. The idea is to insert the egg into your infield as a way to strengthen it and increase feeling.

I got really good at it until one day I decided to wear it out for the day. I was in NYC, walking to meet a friend for lunch. All was well until suddenly I felt the egg moving. My steps got smaller and smaller until I stopped and laid an egg on Fifth Avenue.

There was a load roar. I could see a theater full of smiles. The laughter went on for so long, I nearly forgot where I was in my story.

"I appreciated the wisdom of the experts, but the change for me came when I started listening less to the teachers and more to my body. Instead of positive thinking, I was looking for the positive feeling in my body. My body was asking me to

Go slower

Breathe deeper

Use my voice

Know thyself.

My research became less about orgasm and more about finding ways to keep my body in a balanced state of feeling good—and that had nothing to do with sex.

I found that I was really tracking the sensation that felt good, that was positive in my body, and then following the next positive sensation, and then the next one. I was retraining my body to feel good.

And then I started to do that in life as well. I stopped doing the things in life that didn't feel good or felt like distractions. I stopped hanging out with people who I thought were friends but really weren't.

I started making choices that felt good, that felt true. I was flooding my body with the same feel-good chemicals that are released during orgasm, but I was doing it by just making choices in my daily life that felt good.

I finally won the race by listening to my body, not the doctors or the experts.

The biggest surprise after five years of research?

I'm the healthiest I've ever been. I am never sick.

I'm the most creative I've ever been. I'm getting ready to release my fourth book. I travel the world leading retreats.

And I'm the happiest I've ever been.

I healed my body not just through the medicine of orgasm

But also by creating an orgasmic life and that has absolutely nothing to do with sex.

My mom is here with her book club.

I looked in her direction and placed my hand on my heart.

"Thank you, Mom, for the gift of life.

I love you.

I'm glad I came into the world through your vagina."

As I finished, the room exploded into applause. I stood on the stage, stunned that I had done it, all of it—the research, the writing, and the courage to speak up, especially in the city where most of the damage happened. My heart flickered with light. I smiled in the direction of my mom, hoping that she was smiling too.

After my talk, people lined up to speak to me and thank me for sharing my story. One was a friend from high school I hadn't seen for forty years. Another woman introduced herself as the nurse on call when I delivered my first child, Sam. At the end of the line were many of my longtime friends—Vicki, Amy, Lauren, Bobby, Jenifer, Jeannie—waiting patiently to greet me. Several women approached me with tears in their eyes and thanked me because for the first time they realized nothing was wrong with them. Their inability to orgasm was simply their bodies protecting them in a world that didn't feel safe. They would start their research, too, they said.

After speaking to everyone in line, I went to find my mother, but she was already gone. There were no messages from her on my phone. It brought memories of the last time she heard me speak and left without saying anything.

Earlier the next morning, I received a call from Mom.

"I am still laughing," she said. "After your talk, my book club went out for dinner and talked for several hours about our own experiences around not speaking up. I think you're right—our bodies can hold unexpressed trauma, and later in life we can be misdiagnosed."

I smiled as she continued.

"We're starting your book next week in book club."

TWENTY-FOUR

By the fall of 2017, I'd released three anthologies called *Autobiographies of Our Orgasms,* featuring stories by women and a few men telling the truth about their sensual paths. It was not erotica, although some passages were erotic. It was not self-help, although some stories gave guidance. It was simply women writing the truth of their sex lives, and for many of them, it was the first time to share the intimate details of the most sacred parts of themselves. Unfortunately, so many of our sensual lives began and ended the day we experienced abuse. The physical, mental, and emotional impact of the assaults stays in the body until we make the conscious choice to release it.

The odds are about one in every three women in the world experience sexual assault in their lifetime, over half before the age of eighteen. For the anthologies, it seemed like two of every three stories was about a women's first experience with sex being forced and the common theme of not speaking up. I continued doing book events or writing workshops where women would share their stories out loud. For many, including myself, my voice shook as I read my story even though I had long healed from the trauma. I kept telling my story until my voice stopped shaking. I wanted every woman to know there is nothing wrong with her if she can't feel her orgasm—it was simply her body's way of protecting her. I also wanted her to know that with some dedication and exploration, her orgasm would come to her. Her body would remember because women are wired to feel joy. We are supposed to feel good.

Now, I know it never was about the orgasm; it was about remembering my body as holy no matter what had happened, but that wasn't up to someone else to tell me, it was for me to claim myself.

I traveled all over the world looking for somewhere that felt like home until I remembered the best garden was the one within. If I wasn't blooming, nothing around me would thrive, but I was the one responsible for the watering. I was the home I was waiting for.

One thing I've learned as an activist and advocate for women is the impact of trauma on our bodies. Our bodies don't know the difference between physical, emotional, or mental trauma. As we are being called to speak up and organize, we also need to do it from a place of radical self-care. As Audre Lorde writes: "Caring for myself is not self-indulgence, it is self-preservation, and that is an act of political warfare."

I dedicated three years to cultivating my body through near-daily bliss sessions. There were many days I forgot or was too tired, but the innate wisdom of my cells would seduce me into honoring my sensual being. I knew the sessions were sending feel-good chemicals and hormones that nourished my brain, balanced my cells, and created vitality.

I was the healthiest I'd ever been, I was the most content I'd ever been, and I was in a constant flow of creation. I was also in the most sensual phase of my life.

Technically, I'd remained celibate, refraining from an intimate relationship with another partner, but physically, I didn't experience a lack. A few months earlier, a man in Los Angeles had asked me out. I smiled, knowing he was closer to my oldest son's age.

"I'm fifty-four," I said, trying to chase him away.

"I thought you were closer to forty," he replied. "I'd still love to invite you to dinner."

"I'm a grandmother," I added. "And I'm wearing tennis shoes with orthopedic inserts."

He smiled, looking down at my shoes and then back into my eyes.

"I want to know more about you," he said. "Will you give me your number?"

I shook my head no. In the past, I might have been interested to explore with someone I had no future with, but now I was letting my body guide me, and she said no.

"Then can we follow each other on Instagram?" he said with a smile.

I handed him my cell, and he typed in his name on Instagram and pressed Follow. I later discovered he was the son of a famous actor. As I left him, he said, "If you change your mind, send me a message on Instagram."

I wasn't looking for anyone to please me or fulfill me or complete me, so when I later walked into an event where a man I knew casually was standing, I was confused at the strong reaction from my body. My heart pounded, my pelvis ached, and I had to take a deep breath. There was a flood of moisture in my pussy. He was maybe twenty feet away. We locked eyes and smiled before I turned away. I'd forgotten how to let someone in, even if just for a moment. Later that day, I couldn't stop feeling him in my body, like a force was activated. I decided maybe it was time to release my private bliss sessions and open myself to the possibility of being with a partner. The strong reaction had only happened once before and I hadn't fully trusted my body that time because I was dwelling in a body that wasn't healed. This time, I was living fully in the power of my cells with my body guiding me. I trusted her now with my life.

TWENTY-FIVE

In 2016, scientists at Northwestern University discovered there was a bright light that flashes at the moment of conception. During creation, it's dark until the sperm meets the egg and then suddenly there is light.

The light reminds me of the feeling of seeing a flash of light at the end of a sunset in Miami or a rainbow in the midst of a storm in Indiana. The flash reminds me of the joy of dancing with a circle of women in Zimbabwe or the appreciation for the earth as I hiked through the rice fields in Bali. The flash reminds me of the tenderness of holding my granddaughter, Sunny, for the first time. To me, the flash is love and after 1,000 days without a home, that flash exploded into my heart during the summer of 2017.

It was a sunny afternoon in Miami. I'd walked the beach that morning, taken a swim, and then was lounging in the afternoon sun flooding into the bedroom where I was staying.

I'd taken a shower, and my clothes were off. I rubbed coconut oil onto my body, my tan skin soaking in the moisture. I was planning to dress and work for a few hours, but I felt an ache in my pelvis, so I let my hands glide to my inner thighs, slowly exploring the tops of my legs where my thighs met my genitals. I took a deep breath into my heart and let the exhale dance down my spine. My fingertips were barely touching my skin, but I felt currents of energy lighting up as I traced circles around my vulva.

Slow down even more, I heard, so I did, and felt a mushroom-cloud type of explosion coming from my genitals—not my clit, not my vagina—but from the entire area.

My legs starting vibrating as I inhaled deeper imagining the breath dancing up and down my spine. My arms tingled, and I wasn't too sure if I was even touching myself anymore. I looked down at my breasts and abdomen, noticing the sun sparkling on my skin.

The next inhale came from a place that was deeper than my own body, and a wave of electricity shot through me from my pelvis all the way to my chest. It felt like a lightning bolt cracked open my heart, and as I was jolted upright, a surge of light and ecstasy flooded my heart. In the same way I experienced an orgasm in my genitals, I experienced my heart aching and opening over and over again. I had let go; I couldn't control the moment. My body knew to breathe deeper to pull the warmth of the euphoria into every cell. Tears dripped down my cheeks, and a deep moan came from my throat. The sensations continued. There was so much light around me and within me. At times, it was like I was floating, and my heart was a raft allowing me to feel held, to feel safe, in a sea of love bigger than I'd ever experienced. *Let love in,* I heard. *Let love in.*

I cried for days following that afternoon, knowing for the past three years, I thought I was the one controlling my choices, when really my body had taken me on a pilgrimage back to myself, back to truth, back to love, back to the bright light that flashes at the moment of creation.

A few weeks later, I arrived in Indiana to be with my mom for her next rounds of chemo. She'd been receiving treatment for multiple myeloma in Indianapolis, where one of the best doctors in the world was based not far from where I grew up. I hadn't seen Mom for four months. Every few weeks, I'd get a text from her updating me on the progress of her book club. They read the book together, out loud, at her home and then left the books there until the next gathering. I had a feeling the women, in their late seventies and early eighties, were concerned what their children or grandchildren would think if they found the book on their living room tables, so they left all the copies at my mother's house.

Mom's next round of chemo was just after the total eclipse, which we watched together from her neighborhood. After so many disappointing times for both of us during the past few years, I was happy we were able to get back to love and share this rare moment together, witnessing the light going into darkness and then moving back into light. At the moment of the total eclipse, the light shimmering around the darkness of the moon reminded me of the flash during the moment of conception. For my mom and I, it was a moment of us giving birth to a new way to be with each other.

And then Mom surprised me.

"I remember that day," she said.

"What day?" I asked.

"I remember the day you wrote about in your book," she said, "when the neighbor molested you."

I was stunned. The one thing about sexual assault, especially in childhood, is when the memories do surface, in my case over forty years later, you begin to doubt yourself. In my writing workshops and retreats, I've read so many stories of women finally speaking up about sexual abuse in childhood only to not be believed by the adults in their lives. After all these years, Mom finally remembered.

"I remember Betty showing up to pick you up later that day," Mom said. "But that wasn't unusual. You were always calling your godparents to take you to their home."

I listened, unsure of even what to say.

"And later, I remember finding your dolls hidden in your room," she continued. "You had poked their eyes, ears, and mouth out. Now, I understand it was indication of abuse. It wasn't talked about then."

And that was all she said. We didn't talk about it anymore, and I didn't need to. It was enough that she had the courage to speak up too.

The silence was broken.

TWENTY-SIX

I woke up suddenly feeling like I was going to be sick. *Where was I?* I'd slept in so many different countries, cities, homes, and beds in the past three years that my first thought when I opened my eyes was trying to remember where I was. I looked up at the sky filled with stars. Now I remembered. I was on a houseboat at Lake Ouchita, Arkansas. It was September 2017.

I arrived earlier that day for the wedding celebration of my friend Rochelle. I was excited for the wedding rehearsal the next day. I'd be joined by many of the women in my life who were living as love in action. I was sharing a room on the boat with my dear friend Ingrid Sato, a somatic psychotherapist. The bed was quite small, so I decided to sleep on the top deck so I could fall asleep in the fresh air, letting the stars light my dreams.

All my bliss sessions for the past three years had been in the privacy of a bedroom somewhere in the world, but that night, as I lay alone on the lounger looking up at a galaxy of stars, my hands drifted beneath the blanket and pulled up my black slip. My right hand reached towards my pussy. In just a few minutes my body was vibrating with electric energy until an elixir of pleasure rolled over me—*la petite mort*—another little death. The chemicals released during the orgasm made my head and body drift into a deep sleep.

It was sometime after midnight when I when awoke feeling slightly dizzy and nauseated. The urge to vomit came on strong. Was it food poisoning? We'd eaten pizza for dinner. I got up from the lounger and started to walk to the back of the top deck where there were stairs down to the boat's cabin. After a few steps, my feet got heavy like I was walking in mud. I held onto the rail as I made my way down the stairs, hoping I could make it to the inside bathroom to throw up. I stopped at the bottom of the stairs and sat, feeling like my legs couldn't hold me anymore.

I remember leaning over the side of the boat to vomit.

The next thing I remember is waking up on the deck. I must have collapsed. Fortunately, it was in the direction of the boat instead of the water. How long had I been there? The right side of my cheek was wet and raw. The skin stung where my face had hit the artificial grass carpeting on the rear deck. I tried to get up but couldn't move. It went dark again.

The next time I woke up, I scooted towards the door to the cabin. I opened the door and crawled into the living room. I tried to stand but collapsed again.

I woke up face down on the floor. Ingrid was sleeping in a room maybe twelve feet away. Another couple was sleeping in a room at the back of the boat. I tried to yell, but my throat was closing. I had no voice. It went dark again.

Sometime during the darkness, I remembered. This had happened before. I was in anaphylactic shock. I'd experienced it twice before, but I hadn't had a reaction for twelve years. I'd stopped carrying an Epi-pen a few years ago before because it seemed like my body had outgrown the reaction. I wrote about the first time it happened in my book, *Autobiography of an Orgasm*:

For fun, I once had a woman read my palm. She gazed at my hand for several minutes, tracing the lines with her finger. She told me how many children I would have ("five, but one is different," she said) and how many men I would marry ("three"). I rolled my eyes thinking she's not so good. I'd been married twice in my twenties and didn't plan on another wedding. And, at first, I thought she was wrong about the children, I only had four. And then I remembered my fifth baby died, maybe that was what she meant by one was different.

She said I'd have a long life. Then she stopped and looked closer at a line on my palm. "Have you had your near-death experience yet?"

I looked down at my hand to try and see what she was seeing.

"Ummm, no," I said.

"You will," she said confidently. "Don't worry, you won't die, but it will be the start of a shift in your life."

Four years later, I was in Florida meeting friends for a drink on their boat. My sandals were off, and as I walked through the grass to board the boat, I felt a sting. The electric shock went all the way up my leg. I didn't think much about it as I joined my friends onboard for a glass of champagne. Just as we toasted, a wave of heat flushed through my body. Sweat started pouring from my face, arms and legs.

"I think I'm going to be sick," I said to my friend, Kris.

I could tell from her face that I didn't look good.

"Let me take you inside to the bathroom," she said.

I felt dizzy as I stood up. Kris took my arm to steady me, and we walked the few feet to the cabin of the boat. My heart was racing and pounding like it would break through my chest. My throat was constricting; I couldn't get a breath. I started to get scared when I felt like I was suffocating. I heard Kris's voice yell for help as I hit the floor.

And then it was peaceful. I was floating in white space. I was connected to everything around me, like my body didn't end, it expanded past the skin. All the painful sensations were gone. I could breathe. I wasn't afraid anymore.

I heard voices. They didn't belong to any of my friends, but they sounded like regular voices, as if suddenly there were more people on the boat with us.

"She's not supposed to be here yet," I heard. "She has to go back."

I was content staying right where I was, floating in a space that reminded me of the peace I felt as a child when I lay in the grass and looked at the clouds, connecting to the sky and the earth at the same time. I felt that peace holding my newborn baby, watching a sunset or being surprised by a rainbow. I felt that peace when a favorite song came on the radio or when I was dancing. I felt that peace when I fell in love. In those moments, there was knowingness, a confirmation, of the deeper truths that can only be felt, not learned.

More discussion swirled around me, but none of the voices were talking to me.

I don't know where I am, I thought, but I don't want to leave. My entire being surrendered to whatever would happen next. Both outside and inside my body felt balanced and whole; there was no split or struggle to hide parts of me.

I wanted to ask if I could stay. I turned my head toward the voices to speak. They ignored me. It seemed like they knew what was on my mind: Don't make me go back. It feels so good here.

"She can't stay. She's still supposed to . . . "

And with those words, I suddenly saw Kris and my other friends' faces above me. I was back in my body, lying on the floor and looking up at them. My clothes were drenched with sweat. My breathing was back to normal. Kris helped me sit up and got me a class of water. I was too dazed to tell her what I saw on the other side. A friend took me to the ER and they checked my vitals. The doctor said I had gone into anaphylactic shock from being bitten by a bug.

"You're lucky to be alive," he said.

(Excerpt from *Autobiography of an Orgasm*)

I was awake again. I looked around. I was on the cold floor of the hall bathroom inside the houseboat. How did I get there? My heart was pounding like it was beating its way out of my chest. My abdomen was in excruciating pain. Ingrid was sleeping in the room less than five feet from where I lay. It was two steps up to get to her. The bed was on a platform. I wasn't strong enough to pull myself up. When I tried to call her, nothing came out of my mouth. I thought about lifting my hand and banging it against the shower door that was up against my back. Maybe that would wake her. I couldn't lift my arm. It went dark again.

The next time I came to, I was shivering. My skin was damp from sweating, and now I was shaking from the cold. I pushed myself back into the living room, dragging my legs. Every time I tried to stand, I fell back to the ground. When I got to the couch, I pulled a blanket on top of me. I tried to get warm, but I couldn't.

I remembered the second time I'd experienced anaphylactic shock, not long after the first time. I happened to be in the Miami offices of Janet Galipo, an acupuncturist and BodyTalk practitioner, whose patients travel across the world to see her.

Clients work with Janet as a complement and as an alternative to traditional medicine. I believe she saved my life that day.

On the way to a scheduled appointment with her, I'd felt a bite on my foot as I parked the car. By the time I made it into her office, my heart was racing, and I was ready to faint. She took me into a room and started emergency BodyTalk treatment on me. In her office, I was scared. There were no white lights or dreamy out-of-body experience like the last time. My throat was constricting until it felt like I would suffocate. Janet kept working on me, balancing the cortices of my brain as she asked for someone to call for an ambulance. I didn't need the ambulance. The BodyTalk treatment reminded my body that it knew how to heal, and it did.

Back on the houseboat, I knew each anaphylactic shock experience could be more severe than the last. I knew it could result in death. This time I was alone with no medical attention. My heart raced, and sweat was pouring from my skin. The slip I was wearing was soaked. I couldn't speak but noticed that my throat had stopped constricting.

And then my body remembered.

It started to do what I'd trained it to do the past three years. I started to massage myself—or maybe I imagined I did, because when I tried to move my arms I was unable to control them, as if weights were holding them down, and I was sinking deeper into shock. I silently reminded my body, "You know how to heal" before I dove into the darkness again.

I was in and out of the darkness all night. Every time I was conscious and saw a little light, I said to myself, "You know how to heal."

In the same way that my body went on autopilot and pulled me into my sensual energy the past three years, now I was reminding myself to choose life, not death. Like an injured animal in the wild that knows to take care of itself, I was soothing myself and silently saying, *You know how to heal.*

It continued to get darker. I didn't know if it was the night or in my subconscious. It was quiet on the boat; a calm stillness stayed with me as I continued to repeat, "You know how to heal" like I was planting the seeds of a mantra in my heart just before everything went dark again.

The next time I was conscious, the light was brighter, like a flash.

Where was I?

I looked at the clock across the room. It was 7:10 a.m.

What happened during the night? Was it a dream? I slowly stood up and made my way to the bathroom. I looked in the mirror. The right side of my face was covered in blood, and my hair was stuck in the exposed tissue of a raw wound. I washed my face before I crawled into bed next to Ingrid. She was just waking up. When she saw the blood on my face mixed with tears, she reached out to lay her hands on me like a mother protecting a child.

I was alive.

Ingrid and I took a speedboat and then a car to the hospital for me to be evaluated. I was given a new prescription for an epi-pen. We returned to the houseboat later that day and I went for a swim in the healing waters of Lake Ouchita, which had crystal quartz covering a large part of the lake bottom.

As I spent the next four days celebrating Rochelle's holy union, I was aware of the miracle of my own body's ability to heal through the love I'd been giving it for the past three years, especially after a lifetime of neglect. My exploration of my sensual energy had left my body in a state of wellness that made it possible for my immune system to fight off the toxins that invaded my body during anaphylactic shock. I replaced the poison with love.

My back and legs were covered in bites from the fire ants. It hadn't just been one bite like the previous times my body was sent into anaphylactic shock. This time there were dozens of bites covering my back, shoulders, and thighs. I later discovered a nest of fire ants on the houseboat a few feet from where I'd slept under the stars that night. When my friend Dee found out about my near-death experience, she told me about her grandfather, who was a farmer in West Texas. "He used to tell us it was important to get the newborn calves up and walking as soon as possible after they were born, because a bite from a fire ant could kill them."

Just before Rochelle walked down the aisle to be married, a woman sang the words to a favorite song, "Please Prepare Me to Be a Sanctuary." Tears rolled down my cheeks, through the still-exposed wound from when I collapsed two nights earlier. I knew that during the past three years I had treated my body as a temple, and I believe it saved my life.

TWENTY-SEVEN

I've been living home free for over 1,000 days and it's been one of the biggest gifts of my life. During the past three years, I've lived around the world, being invited to share people's homes and food and conversations.

Someone once told me "to live where you pray best." Now, I remember I can find that home anywhere because my body is my first home. Maybe that's what I needed to remember: to feel more alive in my own body and that my sensual energy contains a life force that becomes a superpower when I need it most.

While I originally planned on a year of private bliss sessions to explore and know my sensual energy, now I'm grateful I slowed down and gave myself three years to release all the toxins and imprints of the history of damage. During the three years, I became the sensual authority on myself by taking my body to places no lover had ever taken me. I also healed a lifetime of assault, neglect, and shame. What I didn't expect was to end up healthier, happier, and more creative.

By tapping into the power of my sensual energy, I experienced sovereignty over my body and over my life. It was my 1,000 day pilgrimage exploring the life force that existed beneath the largest organ on my body, my skin. Early damage had changed the physiology of my body, and then I changed it back.

As a woman and a mother and now an elder, I know that I am a creator beyond giving birth to my children. During a summer retreat in Northern New Mexico, I experienced how Native Americans honor the mother. For the final gathering of the retreat, anyone who was getting married or had experienced great loss was invited to offer a blessing to the others. I stood with the group who would be giving the blessings in the form of a sticky cake called *Tha-Lu* which translates to "a woman's cake." Only initiated women can make this cake for initiated men under specific circumstances. I was offering the "pussy cake" to the masculine as a way for them to eat and embody the feminine. As a ritual, it felt like a conscientious and sacred way to respect and acknowledge the creator, The Mother.

My granddaughter Sunny is a bright light in my world, and she has a little sister due in January of 2018. I'm looking for a home close to Sunny, closer to the light, and I'm making choices that support the voices and the legacy of women in my family.

My son Willie continues to do stand-up in Chicago. Recently, he was invited to do a set at The Laugh Factory, a popular and prestigious stage for comedians. My mom went to the show with me. Willie has become braver in his comedy. I know there were many moments in life that I let him down as a mother. I hope he takes all the painful moments and writes about them or tells a story about them so he can find meaning in the shadows of his life too. The night of his set at The Laugh Factory, he talked about drug use, divorce, and dating choices—both his and his parents'. I've heard Willie do jokes about his father dating the family babysitter. They never got much of a laugh. I always thought it was because our family story seemed too unbelievable to be true. But that night, Willie told it from a new perspective, and it made me fall in love again with the quirkiness of our family, even Ben and Annie. My mom, who was in the midst of chemo treatments, laughed louder and longer than anyone that night, except for maybe me. All these things about our family that we tried to hide were now becoming medicine through our laughter. Willie had taken our family life and turned it into art—into a masterpiece.

I now see that all the death and disappointments of the past few years and throughout my life were an invitation to go deeper into that place of creation to experience that flash of the light over and over again, when out of the darkness, something special is created.

I still haven't been intimate with a partner, but I am ready to explore sharing that part of my life too. I'll listen to my body for the whispers when it's a partner who can be present with my heart. I'll remember to slow down, both for sex and for love. To prepare, I replaced the condoms in my travel bag after realizing they had expired two years ago.

Just like me, my friend Kaci is opening her heart to dating again. She is writing a book about her love story with Jhonny. This past summer, she joined me for my writing retreat at a private chateau in France, and I was humbled when she said, "Our love story has gotten bigger since he died."

The word *planet* means wanderer. Just like the planets, I will continue to wander. I'm even writing the last lines of this book on a plane from Zimbabwe where I witnessed the joy of thousands of Zimbabweans finally speaking up and celebrating after their president was forced to resign. They'd stayed mostly silent for the thirty-seven years of his presidency because speaking up could result in severe consequences. Through it all they kept hope, and their hope finally gave birth to the liberation of their voices and their country.

Lindsay and Tom, who lost their children and home during a fire, are bringing greater awareness to home fire safety. I know their work is saving lives. They joined me on my retreat to Zimbabwe in 2016. A few weeks before our retreat group arrived, a baby elephant named Kantunga died unexpected of a heart issue. When we arrived, the caregivers and community were still grieving, just like Lindsay and Tom. On one of the last nights of the retreat, our group spent the night in the bush with three elephants and their caregivers. One of the eles, Mandebvu, was Kantunga's mother. We made sure to give her some extra love as we fed her before her bedtime.

It was a night to remember. We shared gin-and-tonics at sunset, and dinner was cooked over the campfire. I went to bed earlier than everyone else, smiling as I fell asleep to the sounds of the stories and the laughter of my friends and the caregivers for the elephants (who were also friends). I woke up in the middle of the night not sure where I was. I had cried myself awake, but it wasn't from sadness—it was from happiness. Everyone was asleep. I could hear the elephants eating nearby. I looked up at the galaxy of stars blanketing the African sky and continued to cry; remembering that first trip in 2008 when I arrived in Zimbabwe to adopt a baby and found out she had died. That night in Zimbabwe, I had cried myself to sleep. Now, eight years later, I was crying myself awake. I was exactly where I was supposed to be.

The next morning, as we were packing after breakfast, the elephants and caregivers took off ahead of us so the elephants could eat breakfast along the way. We watched them lumber towards the nearest trees and lift their trunks high to pull down leafy limbs from the tree. Instead of following the other elephants, Mandebvu walked over to Lindsay and Tom and reached out her trunk. And Lindsay and Tom reached for Mandebvu. The rest of us stayed silent as we witnessed three parents grieving their lost boys. In that moment, I saw how love and sadness could coexist. I saw how grief and joy could be dance partners. The answers to my questions were all around me.

I grabbed my backpack and walked out of the silence and towards the morning light.

86990111R00111

Made in the USA
Columbia, SC
09 January 2018